新经典 ENGLISH MAJOR 高等学校英语专业系列教材

英汉交传入门

Gateway to English-Chinese Consecutive Interpreting

邓小文 王海若　　编著

外语教学与研究出版社
FOREIGN LANGUAGE TEACHING AND RESEARCH PRESS
北京 BEIJING

图书在版编目（CIP）数据

英汉交传入门 / 邓小文，王海若编著. -- 北京 ：外语教学与研究出版社，2024.4
新经典高等学校英语专业系列教材
ISBN 978-7-5213-5201-6

Ⅰ. ①英… Ⅱ. ①邓… ②王… Ⅲ. ①英语－口译－高等学校－教材 Ⅳ. ①H315.9

中国国家版本馆 CIP 数据核字 (2024) 第 083447 号

出 版 人　王　芳
项目策划　屈海燕
责任编辑　刘小萌
责任校对　张　阳
封面设计　水长流文化　覃一彪
版式设计　锋尚设计
出版发行　外语教学与研究出版社
社　　址　北京市西三环北路 19 号（100089）
网　　址　https://www.fltrp.com
印　　刷　三河市北燕印装有限公司
开　　本　787×1092　1/16
印　　张　11.5
字　　数　312 千字
版　　次　2024 年 4 月第 1 版
印　　次　2024 年 4 月第 1 次印刷
书　　号　ISBN 978-7-5213-5201-6
定　　价　47.90 元

如有图书采购需求，图书内容或印刷装订等问题，侵权、盗版书籍等线索，请拨打以下电话或关注官方服务号：
客服电话：400 898 7008
官方服务号：微信搜索并关注公众号"外研社官方服务号"
外研社购书网址：https://fltrp.tmall.com

物料号：352010001

前言

　　本教材属本科翻译专业（BTI）交替传译入门教材，旨在系统培养从英语（B语，即外语）译入汉语（A语，即母语）的英汉交替传译能力。本书以口译技能训练为主线，依据社会文化理论（sociocultural theory）视角下的活动理论（activity theory）设计教学活动，辅以相关口译技能理论知识，通过阶段性训练，系统培养英汉交传意识和能力，为下阶段以主题知识为主线的英汉交传能力培养打下坚实的基础。

　　本教材有四大特色：

　　一、本教材以英汉交传技能为核心，不仅告诉读者要练什么（核心英汉交传技能），还列出了怎么练（训练步骤和可能出现的问题）及为什么要练（技能背后的理论和研究），引导学生知其然并知其所以然，帮助他们习得和内化口译技能。学习本教材时，学生可以通过阅读相关研究文章深入了解技能背后的理论，根据练习步骤和要求进行针对性练习，并了解此阶段的常见问题。

　　二、本教材根据编者"英汉交传入门"课程多年的教学经验发展而来，该课程根据社会文化理论视角下的活动理论设计了七大教学活动，分别是：

- 活动1（A1）子技能典型示范和讲解；
- 活动2（A2）教师示范；
- 活动3（A3）学生练习；
- 活动4（A4）篇章口译；
- 活动5（A5）课下小组练习；
- 活动6（A6）口译练习日志；
- 活动7（A7）测试和评价。

　　教材体现了活动1、3、4、6和7，还包括补充阅读、练习方法、练习点评等内容，通过科学的活动设计，循序渐进促进口译初学者掌握英汉交传技能并形成可迁移能力。

　　三、本教材的重心不是英汉交传技能本身，而是如何习得英汉交传技能。前者属于"意识"（awareness），后者是通过练习后获得的"能力"（competence），后者才是口译学习的重点。口译是练出来的，要掌握英汉交传技能，就需要针对性的口译技能练习。

　　恰当、合理的练习材料是实现能力转化的关键。本教材中所有练习材料均由口译授课教师根据口译技能教学的要求精挑细选而来，大部分是真实的英语讲话或演讲原音，声音清晰，语速从稍慢到正常（80~110字/每分钟），形式多样，题材广泛，在课堂教学中使用多年且效果良好。每章的篇章练习与本章讲解的口译技能相匹配，有合理的停顿标示，并配有音频文字稿和参考译文。

四、口译的方向性（directionality）决定了口译思维模式和训练模式的差异。交传课程一般按口译方向分别开设，如英汉交传和汉英交传。对以中文为母语的中国学生来说，由于母语水平和外语（即英语）水平的差异，英汉交传的难点在听和理解，这与译入外语的汉英交传有显著不同，后者的难点更多在于表达。本教材专注于英汉交传技能，通过源语复述和交传练习，深入剖析和发掘英汉交传的特点、难点和训练方法，不仅能够指导学生练习口译技能、了解译员职业特点，也有助于增强他们对英语世界的了解。

本教材可用于一学期的口译教学，也可以自学使用，适用于口译方向本科生和研究生、口译职场人士或口译爱好者。得益于近二十年来国内外口译教学与研究的发展和成熟，我们发展出了本教材同名课程的教学活动，并已在北京外国语大学英语口译教学中使用多年。教材同名课程已在中国高校外语慕课平台（UMOOCs）上线，可配合本教材使用。感谢口译教学同行、专家学者和所有使用本教材的师生。所选材料多来源于网络，在此一并致谢。书中难免存在疏漏，敬请读者批评指正。

邓小文

编写说明

1　适用课程

　　《英汉交传入门》教材是"英汉交传入门"（以下简称"入门"）课程近二十年教学成果之一。该课程是北京外国语大学英语学院翻译本科专业的核心专业必修课程。

　　与培养双语能力为主的教学翻译不同，"入门"属于翻译教学范畴，致力于培养应用型、专业性的职业口译人才，同时着力提升学生的中英双语语言和文化功底、培养娴熟的双语转换能力和宽广的人文知识和素养。根据口译认知过程、口译能力发展和口译学习的特点，"入门"借鉴了语言学、教育学、心理学等领域的研究成果，采用以口译技能训练为主线的（skill-based）主流教学模式，根据社会文化理论视角下的活动理论设计教学活动，系统介绍英汉交传的各项技能，培养和提高学生的英汉口译能力，包括准确而流畅的口头表达能力、举止得当的公共演说能力、准确的数字口译能力、良好的应变能力和心理控制能力，并使他们了解职业译员的基本素质和道德，同时兼顾自主学习能力，为进入下一阶段口译实务课程打下坚实的技能基础。

　　本教材适用于与"入门"相类的本科交传入门课程。通过学习本教材，学生能了解英汉交传的核心子技能、练习方法及相关理论知识，具备一定双语能力和口译能力，能借助笔记准确、流畅、得体地完成一般主题下1~2分钟语段的英文复述或口译，且符合职业规范。此外，学生还能从英语讲话或名人演讲中汲取英语世界的知识和养分，从优秀译员的表现中积累经验和方法，实现译员能力的全面发展。

2　教学设计

　　本教材从教学实践发展而来，体现了基于活动理论的教学设计。社会文化理论描述了人作为主体（subject）如何运用中介工具（mediating artifacts）开展社会活动，以实现对客体（object）的认识（knowing）。活动理论作为其拓展，强调以"活动"为核心范畴，认为社会活动是主体学习和发展的最重要形式，引入共同体（community）、劳动分工（division of labor）和规则（rules）三个概念，形成一个有机的活动系统（Engeström，1987），详见下图：

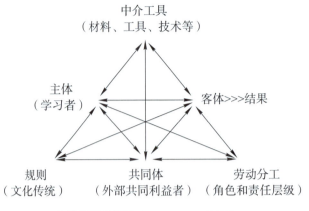

中介工具
（材料、工具、技术等）

主体
（学习者）　　　　　　客体>>>结果

规则　　　　　　共同体　　　　　　劳动分工
（文化传统）　（外部共同利益者）　（角色和责任层级）

人类的活动体系（Engeström, 1987）

从上图可见，主体（即学习者）和客体之间通过中介工具进行调节，从而实现学习结果。这一过程中的角色有共同体，如学生、教师、家长、朋友等；有规则，如教学大纲、教学方法等；还有劳动分工，如课堂上教师与学生分工等。在口译课堂中，口译教学就是语言和认知发展的活动系统，口译教学的任务就是要促使或确保中介作用发生，从而实现培养口译能力这一目标。活动理论对于口译课堂的启示具体包括以下四个方面：

1）口译是一种社会文化实践，口译教学不仅提高口译能力，更注重口译职业素质培养；

2）口译教学过程被设计成活动过程。在此过程中，中介作用、活动和言语活动交织发生，以帮助学生实现口译语言、认知和职业素养协同发展；

3）口译课程要求学生学会感知、诠释和概念化口译技能，涉及复杂的心智活动及问题解决能力培养，如理解、解释、分析、应用、评估和创新；

4）口译能力具有跨学科特点，是可迁移能力，对个人成就和未来职业、专业发展具有促进作用。

3　主要内容

本教材共分为三个阶段：无笔记训练、笔记训练和综合训练，每个阶段都包括若干章口译技能训练和阶段测试和总结。其中，无笔记训练阶段包括五章，训练学生掌握听意不听词、逻辑分析、短期记忆、应对策略等技能。笔记训练阶段包括五章：笔记基本问题、记大意、记大意之间的联系、笔记符号、笔记与表达。综合训练阶段包括三章：跨文化意识、口译中的公共演说能力、表达中的应对。

每章都包含技能解说、训练方法、练习案例点评、篇章练习和补充阅读五大部分。技能解说部分为学生介绍技能本身；训练方法侧重讲解怎么练习本章的口译技能；练习案例点评部分为对学生口译实例的分析；篇章练习部分包含针对该技能的若干个音视频练习材料，可以课上或课下练习使用，并配有生词表、练习说明、音视频文字稿等；补充阅读部分的材料提供每个技能背后的理论和研究。

篇章练习材料都由编者根据口译技能教学的要求精挑细选而来，在教学中使用多年且效果良好。这些内容包括英美人士发表的有影响力的演讲或讲话、大学毕业典礼演讲、国际组织会议发言等，大都语言优美、深刻、富有哲理，将国际视野、家国情怀、文化自信、人格养成等教育内容融入口译教学。通过教师示范、讲解或介绍，学生可以学习优秀译员在口译现场的表现，发现差距，加强修养，实现译员能力全面发展。篇章练习音视频文字稿尽可能与原始语料保持一致，修正了个别语法错误，以删除线表示删去，方括号表示更改，圆括号表示添加。本书依托"U校园智慧云平台"提供篇章练习音频材料及参考译文，方便学生练习和及时复盘。

各阶段末针对此阶段训练中可能出现的问题和解决办法等提供阶段测试和总结。了解普遍存在的问题有助于保持训练的"平常心"，良好的练习心态和状态对口译初学者的重要性不亚于掌握口译技能本身。

本书另外提供了配套在线资源，包括口译训练自评模板、阶段测试和总结的测试题与参考译文、评估与反思填表示例、职业精神和准则以及教学课件，供师生参考和使用。教师可访问HEEP高等英语教学网（https://heep.unipus.cn）下载使用。

4 测试和评估

本教材提供了多种测试和评估模板，采取师生综合评价的方式，即学生自评、同学互评和师生共评，强调学生自主口译学习能力的培养。本教材包含的三个阶段测试和总结就分别采取了这三种评估方式，供师生参考和使用。具体内容包括：

1）无笔记测试：用英文回答关于口译技能的一个问题，2~3分钟；无笔记听一段2分钟英文内容，进行源语复述；学生自评。

2）笔记测试：将纯数字、带单位的数字、含数字的句子和段落分别译为中文；学生互评。

3）综合测试：听一段2~3分钟的英文内容，限时无笔记复述；听3~5分钟的英文内容，可做笔记，将其译成中文；师生共评。

口译技能必须经过大量练习才能内化为能力，课下练习是口译训练的一个有机组成部分（鲍川运，2008），是实现能力培养的关键。建议口译入门课程要求学生每周进行不少于2小时的小组练习，并填写口译练习记录，包括练习具体信息、练习过程、自我评价和改进办法等。学生自行分组进行练习和填写练习记录，教师给予反馈。可参考本教材在线提供的自评模板。

目　录

无笔记训练

第1章 ▶ 听意不听词

一、技能解说

1）口译中的"听"不同于外语学习中的"听"，前者更复杂、更难。

2）口译中的"听"是"积极地听"（active listening）。

3）口译中的"听"要听意思（message），先抓大意，再带细节。

二、训练方法

● 源语复述（retelling）：训练初学者抓大意的能力。

1）如何进行源语复述：
- ✓ 脱离源语外壳
- ✓ 源语转述大意
- ✓ 脑记关键句子
- ✓ 不忘句间联系
- ✓ 运用视觉化等技巧辅助记忆

2）要点提示：
- ✓ 进行源语复述练习时，应边听边分析，体会如何把注意力集中在听信息、理解信息和记忆信息主干上。
- ✓ 源语复述看似简单，但经常出现信息错置、语言不连贯、大脑突然空白等问题，要注意避免。
- ✓ 可以将源语复述的过程类比为"过电影"，如脑中依次浮现听到的第一句的场景或形象等，接着第二句、第三句……直到最后一句，就像脑中放电影一样把整个语段的意思回顾一遍。

三、练习案例点评

──────────────── 案例1 ────────────────

源　语：　　**Lisa:** It has changed my life a lot because I have to look after a baby. I don't get out and do stuff like I used to before. It was a safe delivery, but it was very painful.

Interviewer: You miss school?

    Lisa: Yes, I do.

Interviewer: You like to study?

    Lisa: Yeah.

Interviewer: You'd like to go (to school)?

    Lisa: Yeah, but I don't wanna go back to the same school.

学生复述： It changed my life a lot. It was my first delivery, but it was very painful.

You like study?

Yes.

You like to go to school?

Yes, but I don't wanna go back to the same school any more.

点评

1）这段采访内容有杂音和口音，不容易听清，但还是要尽量听，尽可能从糟糕的源语中听出更多的信息，不能放弃。

2）不要有太多的填充词。

3）采访性对话分别以第一人称视角复述每位讲话者的讲话即可，不需要分别切换两个讲话者视角。

教师评分：90。

案例2

源　语：

    Host: How creative a person are you?

Michael Michalko: Creativity is the ability to look at the same information as everyone else and see something different.

    Host: Michael Michalko, author of the book *Cracking Creativity*, says much of creativity is all in your attitude.

Michael Michalko: (In) one company, we randomly selected employees from different departments and then we told these employees we selected them because we ~~have~~ [had] discovered that they ~~are~~ [were] the most creative employees in the company. Well, within one month the employees that we told they were creative were coming up with and suggesting 90 percent more ideas than the other employees that were told nothing — it was a change in attitude.

学生复述： How creative are you? Creativity is the ability to look at something and come up with information different from others. The author of *Cracking Creativity* says in one case they randomly selected employees from a company and told them they were creative and after a month they were coming up with 90 percent more ideas than employees who were told nothing.

📋 点评

1）这段复述比较完整，大意都出来了，也没有严重的语言错误，比较准确和流畅。

2）讲话者先讲了定义，可以用反差记忆法记住same和different两个信息。第一个关键词是attitude，为了说明这一点，讲话者用了公司的例子。这个例子可以用视觉化的技巧来形象化地记忆，同时记住一个关键数字90%，整个大意就出来了。

3）细节信息，如书名和人名的记忆：前者可记为CC这样的缩略词，又押头韵；人名只记姓，用音对音重复的方法（parroting）记忆具体发音即可。

教师评分：90。

四、篇章练习

生词表

英文	中文
delivery	分娩
Georgetown	乔治敦（圭亚那首都）
Guyana	圭亚那合作共和国（简称圭亚那，位于南美洲北部）
Coordinator of Adolescent Reproductive Health Services	青少年生殖健康服务协调员
psychological trauma	心理创伤
sexually transmitted infections	性传染病
preconceived	预想的，先入为主的
social niceties	社交礼仪
mediate disputes	调解争端
materialistic	物质享乐主义的

1）Teenage pregnancy

练习说明:

1. This is a WHO podcast episode about the risks and consequences of teenage pregnancies.

2. The episode is divided into six segments. Retell the main idea of each segment at the stop signal and record your retelling. Here's a tip for you: Remember that in interviews, the message of a question matches that of its answer.

3. After retelling,

   1) review your recording for quality: Did you get the correct message? Does your retelling contain any language fillers, pauses longer than three seconds, or disorganized information? If so, please try again to address the problems.

   2) think about the following questions: What is the format of such a genre? How much information can you retell from the last segment?

Hostess: You're listening to the WHO podcast. In this episode, we talk about the risks and consequences of teenage pregnancies.

Lisa: It has changed my life a lot because I have to look after a baby. I don't get out and do stuff like I used to before. It was a safe delivery, but it was very painful.

Interviewer: You miss school?

Lisa: Yes, I do.

Interviewer: You like to study?

Lisa: Yeah.

Interviewer: You'd like to go (to school)?

Lisa: Yeah, but I don't wanna go back to the same school. I feel real bad and (I) feel embarrassed.

- -

Hostess: Sixteen-year-old Lisa is from Georgetown in Guyana. The life-changing situation she describes is her unexpected pregnancy. In December 2008, she gave birth to a boy. As a result, she has dropped out of school to stay at home to look after her infant son. They now face many challenges.

However, Lisa's life is made easier, thanks to family and community support. Her mother has helped her through her pregnancy and delivery and Lisa plans to return to school soon. Many teenage girls face serious problems, with about 16 million of them becoming mothers every year. Teenage mothers account for more than 30 births per minute. This is despite the significant drop in teenage pregnancies in most countries in the past 20 to 30 years.

Hostess: Dr. Viviana Mangiaterra from WHO's Department of Making Pregnancy Safer talks about the risks to the health of pregnant teenagers and their babies.

Dr. Mangiaterra: Teenage pregnancy is definitely dangerous for a combination of factors. There are biological factors: The body is not ready; it is a growing body. But also, socio-economic aspects are extremely important as well as the lack of access to services. Children that are born from [to] teenage mother(s) have 50 percent higher risk to die than newborn(s) that are born from [to] older mothers.

Hostess: Pregnancies among teenagers are often unplanned and unwanted. Dr. Elizabeth Mapella is the Coordinator of Adolescent Reproductive Health Services in Tanzania's Ministry of Health and Social Affairs [Welfare]. She tells us more about the consequences for teenage mothers.

Dr. Mapella: A young girl who has been coerced into sex might end up into [with] pregnancy, HIV infection, (and) psychological trauma because this has a long-term impact. Some of them are also not accepted — they are even discriminated.

Looking at those who succeed to go [in going] through that pregnancy, we are also seeing girls after delivery not being able to take care of their children. We are also seeing girls dumping their children because of the social impacts. And looking at their school enrollment and the dropouts, (we find) it is also a social problem for education ensurement [ensuring education].

Hostess: Unlike older mothers, teenage mothers lack education, experience, and income. Dr. Vicki Camacho from WHO's Department of Adolescent Health and Development tells us what kind of help sexually active teenagers should be given.

Dr. Camacho: We need to offer adolescents, boys and girls, different options. And one important option is dual protection, so they get protected against pregnancy but also get protected against sexual [sexually] transmitted infections and HIV/AIDS.

A very key important issue (is that) girls need space for development. Girls need to be empowered to make the right decisions at the right time. If they really decide to have sex, they have to think about what it means and what are the implications of having sex. To do so, they need to have the right information. They need to know where to get services, they need to know what it means ~~having~~ [to have] a baby, and what are the consequences and the implications.

Hostess: That's all for this episode of the WHO podcast. Thanks for listening. If you would like more information on adolescent pregnancy, you can find links on the transcript page of this episode. Look for the podcast link on the home page of the WHO website.

If you have any comments on our podcast or have any suggestions for future health topics, drop us a line.

2）Developing your creativity

练习说明：

1. This is a broadcast titled "How Creative a Person Are You?" in which Michael Michalko, author of a book about creativity, was interviewed.
2. The talk is divided into two segments. Retell the main idea at each stop signal and record your retelling.
3. After retelling,
   1) review your recording for quality: Did you get the correct message? Does your retelling contain any language fillers, pauses longer than three seconds, or disorganized information? If so, please try again to address the problems.
   2) think about the following questions: Did you retell the title of the book and people's names correctly? If not, how can you solve this problem?

Host: How creative a person are you?

Michael Michalko: Creativity is the ability to look at the same information as everyone else and see something different.

Host: Michael Michalko, author of the book *Cracking Creativity*, says much of creativity is all in your attitude.

Michael Michalko: (In) one company, we randomly selected employees from different departments and then we told these employees we selected them because we ~~have~~ [had] discovered that they ~~are~~ [were] the most creative employees in the company. Well, within one month the employees that we told they were creative were coming up with and suggesting 90 percent more ideas than the other employees who were told nothing — it was a change in attitude.

Host: Michael says real creative thinking isn't just coming up with that one great idea.

Michael Michalko: One of the most common characteristics of creative thinkers is quantity. All geniuses produce. They produce incredible quantities of ideas. And one way to get yourself to produce that quantity of ideas is to give yourself an idea quota. Whenever you're looking for an idea, give yourself an idea quota of, say, 50 ideas. Thomas Edison, when he hired his assistant, would always give him an idea quota and an invention quota. His own invention quota was one major invention every six months and one minor invention every 10 weeks.

3）Characteristics of Americans

练习说明：

1. This is a talk about characteristics of the American people. Brainstorm before listening: If you are asked to describe Americans, what would you say?
2. The talk is divided into five segments. Retell the message at the stop signals and record your retelling.
3. After retelling,
   1) review your recording for quality: Did you get the correct message? Does your retelling contain any language fillers, pauses longer than three seconds, or disorganized information? If so, please try again to address the problems.
   2) think about the following questions:
      - What is the main idea of this talk? What are the subordinate arguments?
      - Did you find any words difficult to understand but finally figure them out by putting them back into the context?

You certainly have heard stories, good or bad, about American people. You also probably have preconceived ideas from having met Americans before or from films and television programs that color your impression of what Americans are and what they do. However, American society is enormously diverse and complex and cannot be reduced only to a few stories or stereotypes. Important differences exist between geographical regions, between rural and urban areas, and between social classes. In addition, the presence of millions of immigrants who came to the United States from all corners of the world with their own culture and values adds even more variety and flavor to American life.

There are certain characteristics that represent typical Americans. The first is individuality.

Individuality

Probably above everything else, Americans consider themselves individuals. There are strong family ties and strong loyalties to groups, but individuality and individual rights are most important. If this seems like a selfish attitude, it also leads Americans to an honest respect for other individuals.

Related to this respect for individuality are American characteristics of independence and self-reliance. From an early age, children are taught to "stand on their own two feet," an idiom meaning to be independent. Most U.S. students choose their own classes, select their own majors, follow their own careers, arrange their own marriages, and so on, instead of adhering to the wishes of their parents.

Honesty and frankness are two more aspects of American individuality, and they are more important to Americans than personal honor. Americans may seem direct at times, and in polite conversations they may bring up topics and issues that you find embarrassing, controversial, or even offensive. Americans are quick to get to the point and do not spend much time on social niceties. This directness encourages Americans to talk over disagreements and to try to fix up misunderstandings themselves, rather than ask a third party to mediate disputes.

Again, "individuality" is the key word when describing Americans, whether it is their personalities or their style of dress. Generally though, Americans like to dress and entertain informally and treat each other in a very informal way, even when there is a great difference in age or social standing. Students and professors often call each other by their first names. International students may consider this informality disrespectful, even rude, but it is part of American culture. Although there are times when Americans are respectful of, and even sentimental about, tradition, in general there is little concern for traditional social rules.

Competitiveness

Americans place a high value on achievement, and this leads them to constantly compete against each other. You will find friendly, and not-so-friendly, competition everywhere. Americans can also be obsessed with records of achievement in sports, in business, or even in more ordinary things. Books and movies, for example, are sometimes judged not so much on quality but on how many copies are sold or on how many dollars of profit are realized. In the university as well, emphasis is placed on achievement, on grades, and on one's grade point average, GPA.

On the other hand, even if Americans are often competitive, they also have a good sense of teamwork and of cooperating with others to achieve a specific goal.

Measuring success

Americans are often accused of being materialistic and driven to succeed. How much money a person has, how much profit a business deal makes, or how many material goods an individual accumulates is often their definition of success. This goes back to American competitiveness. Most Americans keep some kind of appointment calendar and live according to schedules. They always strive to be on time for appointments. To international students, American students seem to always be in a hurry, and this often makes them appear rude. However, this attitude makes Americans efficient, and they usually are able to get many things done, in part, by following their schedules.

Many Americans, however, do not agree with this definition of success; they enjoy life's simple pleasures and are neither overly ambitious nor aggressive. Many Americans are materially successful and still have time to appreciate the cultural, spiritual, and human aspects of life.

五、补充阅读

1）Jones, R. (1998). *Conference Interpreting Explained*. Manchester: St. Jerome Publishing.

2）雷天放，陈菁. 口译教程 [M]. 上海：上海外语教育出版社，2006.

3）刘敏华. 逐步口译与笔记：理论、实践与教学 [M]. 台北：书林出版有限公司，2008.

第2章 ▶ 逻辑分析

一、技能解说

1）逻辑分析（logical analysis）是指对听到的信息进行分析，属于语义层面的深度处理（deep-processing），目的是找到信息之间的逻辑关系，从而有利于短期记忆（short-term memory）。

2）逻辑分析可分为竖状（vertical）和横状（horizontal）两种。前者是总—分层级式逻辑关系，后者包括分类关系、因果关系、对比和类比关系、时空关系、程度、提出问题—解决问题等多种关系形式。

3）论述性讲话（argumentation）多为竖状逻辑，描述性讲话（description）和叙述性讲话（narration）多为横状逻辑，有的讲话可能糅合了多种逻辑关系。

二、训练方法

● 大意复述（gist retelling）

1）练习要求：

✓ 听完信息能抓住源语讲话的框架，复述的逻辑清楚，记忆无重大漏洞。

2）要点提示：

✓ 口译的"听"一定要"积极"，如预测讲话者下一点讲什么。预测（anticipation）能降低听和记忆的负担。运用逻辑分析可以帮助预测。

✓ 边听边进行逻辑分析，整理听到的内容并将其填到自己的分析框架里。

三、练习案例点评

—————————————— 案例1 ——————————————

源　　语：　　　　　　　**Host:** Knowing how to disagree gracefully is important.

Meryl Runion: And what that means is that we can say — "OK, I can see how you can see it that way. I see you feel strongly about this. I don't blame you for being upset." — something that acknowledges their situation even though we know that there's more to the story. A lot of times if we can just acknowledge people, it calms them down enough ~~that~~ [and] then they can be more rational and reasonable.

Host: Often when you're dealing with someone who is upset, they need to talk.

Meryl Runion: And so one of my favorite phrases is simply, "Tell me more." If I can just say "Tell me more," what happens is they open up and we get to a place where we can find resolution.

学生复述： To speak with power also means you need to know how to disagree with someone gracefully. The CEO also told me … she often said, "You feel strong about this and I don't blame you for it. I know you are upset but I can understand you." She thinks … people should acknowledge someone's contribution and when people are upset, they need to be encouraged to tell more, so the CEO also told me whenever people feel upset, she told them to tell her more and they could find common ground for a resolution.

📖 点评

1）基本大意概括出来了，但出现了若干次停顿和重复，听感不好且不易理解。

2）人称关系不明，复述时视角和时态来回切换，还出现了意义重复。在最后一句话中，need to be encouraged to tell more把源语变成了转述。Tell me more是讲话者自己说的原话，不是她从别人那里听说的，复述时应站在讲话者的视角。

教师评分：75。

案例2

源　　语： **Lebronze Davis:** There were nine of us at home at one time. All the boys ~~was~~ [were] in one room. We had two beds: Two slept at the head (and) two slept at the feet. And there was one thing about ~~them~~ [their] feet — you washed ~~them~~ [their] feet before you went to bed.

Arguster Davis: We only had one cash crop, which was cotton, and we were just breaking even. You had a hole in your jeans — Mama'd put a patch on it.

Lebronze Davis: … patch on it, and you kept right on going.

Arguster Davis: Keep right on going.

Lebronze Davis: Kids today … They take jeans out, hang them on the line, and shoot them to put holes in them.

Arguster Davis: My first lesson in economics — Daddy taught it to me. We had worked and made a little extra money, and we wanted to go to the fair. I had made six dollars. Six dollars, man — I was on top of the world. I played games. I ate cotton candy. I came back home, and Daddy asked me, "Boy, how much money did you spend at the fair?" And I just held my head down and said, "Daddy, I spent it all." He said, "Boy, you spent all your money, and haircuts (have) gone up to 75 cents." So I always keep me enough money to get me a haircut.

Lebronze Davis: Daddy was warm. If he got it, he'd give it to you. If he didn't have it, he would tell you how to get it.

学生复述： There were nine of us at home. All the boys stay in one room with only two beds. I got a hole in my jeans and Mom put a patch on it. My first lesson in economics is taught by Daddy. When I had made an extra six dollars money, I went to the fair and spend it all. But Dad told me the haircut has risen to 75 cents. So from him I learned that I should always leave enough money for haircuts. If Dad has something, he will give; if not, he will teach me how to get it.

点评

1. 源语中虽有两个人共同讲述同一话题，但不需要转换视角，用第一人称复述观点即可。这段复述整体表现不错，将听懂的内容用自己的语言表达出来，虽有部分错漏，但胜在表述比较流畅。

2. 复述存在细节遗漏，比如Kids today…这一句，又比如关于wash feet的笑点。

3. 还有若干明显语法错误，如stay in one room、is taught by Daddy、spend it all、has risen、will give等都应该用过去时。

教师评分：85。

四、篇章练习

生词表

英文	中文
restraining device	固定件，固位器
three-point lap and shoulder seat belt	三点式腰部及肩部安全带

（待续）

（续表）

英文	中文
abdomen	腹部
buckle	搭扣，带扣
strap	带子
hip	髋部
Royal Swedish Academy of Engineering Sciences	瑞典皇家工程科学院
cash crop	经济作物
syrup mill	糖浆厂
millet	黍，小米，粟

1）Seat belts

练习说明：

1. This is a broadcast introducing the development of seat belts. Anticipate its main topics and logical framework before listening.

2. It is divided into three segments. Retell at each stop signal and record your retelling.

3. After retelling,

   1) review your recording for quality: Did you get the correct message? Does your retelling contain any language fillers, pauses longer than three seconds, or disorganized information? If so, please try again to address the problems.

   2) think about the following questions: There are many names and years mentioned in this broadcast. How did you deal with them in your retelling? Can you think of some ways to memorize them?

Most cars have seat belts as part of their equipment. Seat belts protect drivers and passengers in case of accident. They also reduce the effect of a crash on the body. Safety experts estimate that the restraining devices save more than 4,000 lives a year in the United States alone. Worldwide, some experts say, the devices have protected up to a million people.

The first seat belt was said to have been created in the 1800s by George Cayley of England. He is remembered for many inventions, especially for early "flying machines."

The United States first recognized the invention of an automobile seat belt in 1885. The government gave a patent to Edward J. Claghorn of New York City so that others would not copy his invention. Claghorn called the device a Safety-Belt. It was said to include hooks and other attachments for securing the person to a fixed object.

Other inventors followed with different versions of the seat belt. But more than 70 years passed before the current, widely used seat belt was developed. It resulted from the work of a Swedish engineer, Nils Bohlin. His three-point lap and shoulder seat belt first appeared on cars in Europe more than 50 years ago.

Bohlin was born in Sweden in 1920. After completing college, he designed seats for the Swedish aircraft industry. The seats were built for the pilot to escape from an airplane in case of disaster. Bohlin's work with planes showed him what could happen in a crash at high speed. In 1958, Bohlin brought that knowledge to the Swedish car manufacturer Volvo. He was the company's first chief safety engineer.

At the time, most safety belts in cars crossed the body over the abdomen. A buckle held the restraints in place. But the position of the buckle often caused severe injuries in bad crashes.

Nils Bohlin recognized that both the upper and lower body needed to be held securely in place. His invention contained a cloth strap that was placed across the chest and another strap across the hips. The design joined the straps next to the hip.

Volvo was the first automobile manufacturer to offer the modern seat belt as a permanent addition to its cars. It also provided use of Nils Bohlin's design to other carmakers.

The Swedish engineer won many honors for his seat belt. He received a gold medal from the Royal Swedish Academy of Engineering Sciences in 1995.

2）Speaking with power

练习说明：

1. This excerpt records a podcast that interviewed Meryl Runion, author of the book *Power Phrases!*.
2. The excerpt is divided into two segments. Retell at each stop signal and record your retelling.
3. After retelling,
   1) review your recording for quality: Did you get the correct message? Does your retelling contain any language fillers, pauses longer than three seconds, or disorganized information? If so, please try again and address the problems.
   2) think about the following questions: How did you retell direction quotations in this talk? Are there any better ways to deal with them?

Host: When you're talking to people, using the right phrases at the right time can make you a powerful communicator.

Meryl Runion: One of my favorite power phrases is one that someone shared with me at a seminar I was teaching. It was a customer service situation and someone was being very hostile toward her.

Host: (This is) Meryl Runion, author of the book *Power Phrases!*.

Meryl Runion: Here's what she said. She said, "I am very concerned about your problem and when you speak to me this way I find it difficult to focus on a solution." So she addressed the situation, ~~that~~ [which] sent the message to him that it was in his interest to speak with her in a more responsible manner.

- -

Host: Knowing how to disagree gracefully is important.

Meryl Runion: And what that means is that we can say — "OK, I can see how you can see it that way. I see you feel strongly about this. I don't blame you for being upset." — something that acknowledges their situation even though we know that there's more to the story. A lot of times if we can just acknowledge people, it calms them down enough ~~that~~ [and] then they can be more rational and reasonable.

Host: Often when you're dealing with someone who is upset, they need to talk.

Meryl Runion: And so one of my favorite phrases is simply "Tell me more." If I can just say "Tell me more," what happens is they open up and we get to a place where we can find resolution.

- -

3）Brothers from Wetumpka, Alabama, remembering their father

练习说明：

1. This is an episode of a radio program called StoryCorps. Arguster and Lebronze Davis grew up on their family's farm in Wetumpka, Alabama, U.S. The brothers came to StoryCorps to talk about their 1950s childhood and their dad. Brainstorm before listening: What do people usually talk about when remembering their fathers? What do you think the two brothers are going to talk about?

2. The episode is divided into two segments. Retell the main idea of each segment at the stop signal and record your retelling.
3. After retelling,
   1) review your recording for quality: Did you get the correct message? Does your retelling contain any language fillers, pauses longer than three seconds, or disorganized information? If so, please try again to address the problems.
   2) think about the following questions:
      • Did you hear the background music when listening? Did it help you better understand their talk or distract you instead? Why? How did you cope with it?
      • What is the logical flow of this talk?

Lebronze Davis: There were nine of us at home at one time. All the boys ~~was~~ [were] in one room. We had two beds: Two slept at the head (and) two slept at the feet. And there was one thing about ~~them~~ [their] feet — you washed ~~them~~ [their] feet before you went to bed.

Arguster Davis: We only had one cash crop, which was cotton, and we were just breaking even. You had a hole in your jeans — Mama'd put a patch on it.
Lebronze Davis: … patch on it, and you kept right on going.
Arguster Davis: Keep right on going.
Lebronze Davis: Kids today … They take jeans out, hang them on the line, and shoot them to put holes in them.

Arguster Davis: My first lesson in economics — Daddy taught it to me. We had worked and made a little extra money, and we wanted to go to the fair. I had made six dollars. Six dollars, man — I was on top of the world. I played games. I ate cotton candy. I came back home, and Daddy asked me, "Boy, how much money did you spend at the fair?" And I just held my head down and said, "Daddy, I spent it all." He said, "Boy, you spent all your money, and haircuts (have) gone up to 75 cents." So I always keep me enough money to get me a haircut.

Lebronze Davis: Daddy was warm. If he got it, he'd give it to you. If he didn't have it, he would tell you how to get it.

Arguster Davis: You remember when Daddy started the syrup mill?
Lebronze Davis: Yes.
Arguster Davis: Yes. And people in the community would bring their cane and millet for us to grind up and make syrup. And people would pay with buckets of syrup. I said,

"Daddy, why don't you let these people pay you? Because we got enough syrup to last us for a long time." And he looked at me, and he said, "Son, these people don't have no money to pay. That's the only way they can pay."

Lebronze Davis: Daddy taught us all how to do the right thing and wanted us to do the right thing.

Arguster Davis: He kept me out of school one day because he was delivering lumber. The directions that were given to him were not very clear. And since Daddy — you know, he only went to the third grade — uh, he couldn't read the address. And I said, "I'll help you, Daddy." I couldn't have been no more than eight or ten years old. It was just heartbreaking. You know, there are things that I try to pass on to my son. There's only two things in life a person actually owns, and that is his name and his word. And in his own way, that's what Daddy left me with.

五、补充阅读

1）雷天放，陈菁. 口译教程 [M]. 上海：上海外语教育出版社，2006.

2）刘敏华. 逐步口译与笔记：理论、实践与教学 [M]. 台北：书林出版有限公司，2008.

3）仲伟合. 英语口译教程 [M]. 北京：高等教育出版社，2006.

第3章 ▶ 短期记忆-1

一、技能解说

1）好的译员需要良好的记忆，来记住听到的信息并用另一种语言表达出来。记忆可以分为短期记忆（short-term memory, STM）和长期记忆（long-term memory, LTM）。短期记忆只能保持较短时间，不产生神经回路。长期记忆通过神经回路来存储信息，可以在几周、几个月甚至几年后提取。

2）丹尼尔·吉尔（Daniel Gile）将交替传译分为两个阶段，用公式表达如下：

$$\textbf{\textit{Phase One: I = L + M + N}}$$
$$\textbf{\textit{Phase Two: I = Rem + Read + P}}$$

其中M就是短期记忆，Rem是回忆短期记忆的内容。

在第一阶段中，译员听懂（L, listening and analysis），然后产生短期记忆（M, short-term memory operations），并做笔记（N, note-taking）。在第二阶段中，译员先借助笔记（Read, note-reading）回忆起短期记忆的内容（Rem, remembering），最后才产出（P, production）。

3）短期记忆有四个特点：需要注意力；需要解码声音、图片和意义；会有信息遗失；需要提取才能回忆。

二、训练方法

- 源语或译语复述

1）练习要求：

- ✓ 掌握如何听信息，在大意框架清晰的基础上逐渐增加细节。注意训练强记听到的信息内容的能力，能够在听完后做质量较高的复述或综述。
- ✓ 英文语音材料每段长度从0.5~1分钟逐渐过渡到1.5~2分钟。

2）要点提示：

- ✓ 灵活运用分类、归类、对比、描写、归纳、抽象化等方式记忆源语信息。
- ✓ 体会在没有语言障碍的前提下如何听，并运用逻辑分析技能记忆听到的内容；体会短期记忆的特点，以及逻辑分析对记忆的重要性。

- 影子练习：边听源语边进行源语复述，稍微滞后3~5个词，每说完一段后暂停并复述大意。
- 干扰练习：练习在动作、声音等各种干扰源影响下，集中注意力听并记忆。

三、练习案例点评

———————————— 案例1 ————————————

源　　语：Electronic devices are changing the way people listen to music. But studies show the devices may be causing hearing loss in many people. Some experts say people may be playing them too loud and for too long.

Researchers from Zogby International did a study for the American Speech-Language-Hearing Association. It involved 300 high school students and 1,000 adults. They were asked about their use of portable music devices. Some of the most popular are Apple Computer's iPod, CD players, and portable laptop computers.

学生复述：Electronic devices are changing the way people listen to music. A study showed that the devices may cause hearing loss. It also showed that people use the electronic devices to listen to music too loud and for too long. Zombie Research did a study for an institution that involves about 300 high school students and 1,000 adults … who were asked about their use about portable music devices … And they said, they use Apple Computer iPod, CD players, and laptop computers, most often.

📖 点评

1）大意都复述出来了，但仍有一些信息错漏，还有几处明显停顿，不够流畅。

2）两个机构Zogby International和American Speech-Language-Hearing Association没复述出来，可以使用缩略语记忆法记为ZI和ASHA。

3）注意时态。比如，描述Zogby International所做的研究时，有些句子用现在时，有些用过去时，应统一为过去时。

4）It also showed that people use the electronic devices to listen to music too loud and for too long这样的句子略显啰嗦。

5）有信息错误，too loud and for too long不是出自研究结果，而是来自专家的观点。

6）最后列举前有明显停顿，说明当时没分析出逻辑框架，而是直接记忆了具体内容。除了关键信息，还要注意记忆逻辑联系。

教师评分：85。

源　语： Experts at the Mayo Clinic in Minnesota say any sound above 90 decibels for long periods may cause some hearing loss. But most portable music players can produce sounds up to 120 decibels.

The American Speech-Language-Hearing Association is working with manufacturers and government officials on setting rules for use of portable music devices. The group says the best way to protect your hearing is to reduce the volume, limit listening time, and ~~using~~ [use] earphones that block out foreign noises.

学生复述： Experts from the clinic said that over 90 decibel would damage people's hearing. But the portable music players people use can play music over 100 decibel. So the hearing … errr … listening association … errr … combined with the American government and the manufacture to set the rules … emm … for the portable music player … errr … the decibel of the portable music player. Emm … the way people can protect their hearing is to reduce the volume, limited the listening time, and prevent the foreign noises.

点评

1）信息大体上正确，逻辑比较完整，但存在较多信息和表达上的问题。

2）复述里有一个数字错误，把120记成了100。

3）第三句多次出现了填充词；还有一次完全没有必要的重复，之前的表达已经正确地传达出来了信息，就无需自我修正了。

4）存在一些语法错误，如：decibel没有用复数，最后一句中limited应为limit。

教师评分：75。

四、篇章练习

生词表

英文	中文
portable	便携的
hearing loss	听觉损失，听觉障碍
Zogby International	佐格比国际公司（一家美国民调机构）

（待续）

英文	中文
American Speech-Language-Hearing Association, ASHA	美国言语语言听力学会
earbuds	耳塞式耳机
Mayo Clinic	梅奥医学中心
decibel	分贝
birth control	节育，避孕
two-parent family	双亲家庭
out of wedlock	非婚生的
episodic memory	情景记忆
semantic memory	语义记忆
factual memory	事实记忆
encoding	编码
consolidation	巩固，强化
olfactory	嗅觉的
neurological	神经学的
Alzheimer's, Alzheimer's disease, AD	阿尔茨海默病
schizophrenia	精神分裂症
autism	孤独症
impaired	受损的
National Health Service, NHS	英国国家医疗服务体系

1）Portable music players

练习说明：

1. This talk discusses portable music players and their link to hearing loss. Can you guess what contents might be covered in this talk? What elements will possibly appear in this talk, such as numbers and proper names?

2. The talk is divided into four segments. Retell the message at the end of each segment and record your retelling.

3. After retelling, assess the quality of your recording considering how you should memorize the main ideas and sub-ideas.

Electronic devices are changing the way people listen to music. But studies show the devices may be causing hearing loss in many people. Some experts say people may be playing them too loud and for too long.

Researchers from Zogby International did a study for the American Speech-Language-Hearing Association. It involved 300 high school students and 1,000 adults. They were asked about their use of portable music devices. Some of the most popular are Apple Computer's iPod, CD players, and portable laptop computers.

Forty percent of students and adults said they set the sound levels, or volume, at "high" on their iPods. But students were two times more likely to play the music at a very loud volume. More than half of the students said they would probably not limit their listening time. And about a third said they were not likely to reduce the volume.

The study found that more than half of the students and less than 40 percent of the adults had at least one kind of hearing loss. Some reported difficulty hearing parts of a discussion between two people. Others said they had to raise volume controls on a television or radio to hear it better. And, some experienced ringing in their ears or other noises.

Hearing experts say part of the problem is the listening equipment people are using. They say large earphones that cover the whole ear are probably safer than the smaller earbuds that come with most music players. Earbuds are thought to be less effective than earphones in blocking out foreign noises.

Hearing loss may not be apparent for years. But once it happens, it is permanent. About 30 million Americans have some hearing loss. One third of them lost their hearing as a result of loud noises.

Experts at the Mayo Clinic in Minnesota say any sound above 90 decibels for long periods may cause some hearing loss. But most portable music players can produce sounds up to 120 decibels.

The American Speech-Language-Hearing Association is working with manufacturers and government officials on setting rules for use of portable music devices. The group says the best way to protect your hearing is to reduce the volume, limit listening time, and using [use] earphones that block out foreign noises.

2）American families

练习说明：

1. This is a talk on American families. It is divided into six segments. Retell at each stop signal and record your retelling.
2. After retelling,
   1) review your recording for quality: Did you get the correct message? Does your retelling contain any language fillers, pauses longer than three seconds, or disorganized information? If so, try again and address the problems.
   2) think about the following questions: What is the logic frame of this talk? What are the main ideas and sub-ideas? How should you link these ideas and memorize them?

Good morning, I would like to talk to you today about the American family.

Many Americans formed their idea of family life in the 1950s. But that kind of American family has become increasingly less common in the last 30 years.

Beginning in the 1950s, a wave of social change swept through America. Almost every American family was affected. Historians say the American family has changed more rapidly in the last 30 years than in any other time period.

Social historians say the most far-reaching change in the family has resulted from changes in women's work. A majority of married women in the United States no longer stay at home all day to cook, clean, and raise children. They now have paid jobs outside their homes. So, their young children spend at least part of the day in a child-care center.

Changes in the family also resulted from changes in marriage traditions. During the 1960s, many young men and women began to live together without being legally married. Some had children. They were a family, but not in the traditional sense. At the same time, more people ended their marriage if it was unhappy. The rate of divorce in the United States increased by more than three times in about 20 years. And finally, birth control became more acceptable. Fewer babies were born. The birth rate fell to its lowest point ever in the history of the nation.

With divorce and fewer babies, American families got smaller. They began to look less and less like families in television programs. More families were being raised by a single mother or father. More two-parent families contained children from a husband's or wife's former marriage. More families were made up of three women — a woman who had never gotten married who had a child, a daughter out of wedlock, living with a grandmother or aunt.

Andrew Cherlin, a professor of social science at Johns Hopkins University in Maryland, is a leading expert on families. Mr. Cherlin says changes in the American family began with economic and population changes in the 19th century.

People began buying the things they needed, instead of making them at home. The birth rate went down as the nation became more industrial. Then, after World War II, the economy grew quickly. There were many jobs. Having less to do at home, married women went to work at those jobs. Their earnings helped pay for their families' clothes, education, and holidays.

Social scientists say female employment also removed an important reason for marriage. In the past, women needed husbands to survive economically. And men needed wives to cook for them and make their clothes.

Today, women do not need husbands to survive economically. They can earn their own money. And men do not need wives. They can buy what they need in stores. Because of this, social scientists say that marriages today are based less on economy. Instead, they are based more on the desire for love and friendship, and the desire to create a family.

Social scientists say the high divorce rate does not mean that people have rejected marriage. They note that three out of four divorced people marry again. And most do so within a few years. As population expert Paul Glick says, "Americans like to live in the married way."

More than 90 percent of Americans will marry at some time in their lives. Recent studies by government researchers show that the divorce rate in the United States is still one of the highest in the world. But it has been falling. The rate in 1986 was lower than it had been since 1975. Social scientists say this is happening because more people recognize that divorce is not always the best way to solve marriage problems.

At the same time, public opinion studies show that the great majority of Americans are very happy with their families and marriages. And most American children say they believe that their parents are doing a good job of raising them.

Some people might wish that the family would return to what it was like in the 1950s. Experts say there is no sign that this will happen.

Arthur Norton, a government population expert, says the changes in the American family are real, and they are going to stay, because they have become part of American life. Thank you very much.

3) Episodic memory

练习说明：

1. This talk focuses on episodic memory. What comes to mind when you think of this topic? Brainstorm before listening: Anticipate its main ideas and logic frame as far as possible.
2. The talk is divided into four segments. Retell the message at each stop signal and record your retelling.
3. After retelling, review your recording for quality and think about the following questions: How did you use the skills of categorization, contrast, or visualization to help you memorize the main ideas and sub-ideas? What other memory techniques did you use?

Today we'll be continuing the series of lectures on memory by focusing on what is called episodic memory and what can happen if this is not working properly.

Episodic memory refers to the memory of an event or episode. Episodic memories allow us to mentally travel back in time to an event from the past. Episodic memories include various details about these events, for example, when an event happened and other information such as the location. To help understand this concept, try to remember the last time you ate dinner at a restaurant. The ability to remember where you ate, who you were with, and the items you ordered are all features of an episodic memory.

Episodic memory is distinct from another type of memory called semantic memory. This is the type of factual memory that we have in common with everyone else: That is your general knowledge of the world. To build upon a previous example, remembering where you parked your car is an example of episodic memory, but your understanding of what a car is and (that of) how an engine works are examples of semantic memory. Unlike episodic memory, semantic memory isn't dependent on recalling personal experiences.

Episodic memory can be thought of as a process with several different steps of memory processing: encoding, consolidation, and retrieval. The initial step is called encoding. This involves the process of receiving and registering information, which is necessary for creating memories of information or events that you experience. The degree to which you can successfully encode information depends on the level of attention you give to an event while it's actually happening. Being distracted can make effective encoding very difficult. Encoding of episodic memories is also influenced by how you process the event. For example, if you were introduced to someone called Charlie, you might make the connection that your uncle has the same name.

Future recollection of Charlie's name is much easier if you have a strategy to help you encode it.

Memory consolidation, the next step in forming an episodic memory, is the process by which memories of encoded information are strengthened, stabilized, and stored to facilitate later retrieval. Consolidation is most effective when the information being stored can be linked to an existing network of information. Consolidation makes it possible for you to store memories for later retrieval indefinitely. Forming strong memories depends on the frequency with which you try to retrieve them. Memories can fade or become harder to retrieve if they aren't used very often.

The last step in forming episodic memories is called retrieval, which is the conscious recollection of encoded information. Retrieving information from episodic memory depends upon semantic, olfactory, auditory, and visual factors. These help episodic memory retrieval by acting as a prompt. For example, when recalling where you parked your car, you may use the color of a sign close to where you parked. You actually have to mentally travel back to the moment you parked.

There are a wide range of neurological diseases and conditions that can affect episodic memory. These range from Alzheimer's to schizophrenia to autism. An impairment of episodic memory can have a profound effect on individuals' lives. For example, the symptoms of schizophrenia can be reasonably well controlled by medication. However, patients' episodic memory may still be impaired and so they are often unable to return to university or work. Recent studies have shown that computer-assisted games designed to keep the brain active can help improve their episodic memory.

Episodic memories can help people connect with others, for instance by sharing intimate details about their past: something individuals with autism often have problems with. This may be caused by an absence of a sense of self. This is essential for the storage of episodic memory, and has been found to be impaired in children with autism. Research has shown that treatments that improve memory may also have a positive impact on children's social development. One study looked at …

4）The Queen's broadcast to the U.K. and the Commonwealth on coronavirus

练习说明：

1. This is the Queen's message to all British people and the Commonwealth amid COVID-19. Predict its content before you listen and retell the message.
2. The material is divided into eight segments. Record your retelling at each stop signal.
3. After retelling, review your recording for quality and think about the following questions: What kind of information turned out to be difficult for you to remember, and why? What memory techniques can be used to solve the problem?

I am speaking to you at what I know is an increasingly challenging time, a time of disruption in the life of our country: a disruption that has brought grief to some, financial difficulties to many, and enormous changes to the daily lives of us all.

I want to thank everyone on the NHS front line, as well as care workers and those carrying out essential roles, who selflessly continue their day-to-day duties outside the home in support of us all.

I am sure the nation will join me in assuring you that what you do is appreciated and every hour of your hard work brings us closer to a return to more normal times.

I also want to thank those of you who are staying at home, thereby helping to protect the vulnerable and sparing many families the pain already felt by those who have lost loved ones.

Together we are tackling this disease, and I want to reassure you that if we remain united and resolute, then we will overcome it.

I hope in the years to come everyone will be able to take pride in how they responded to this challenge. And those who come after us will say the Britons of this generation were as strong as any.

That the attributes of self-discipline, of quiet good-humored resolve, and of fellow-feeling still characterize this country. The pride in who we are is not a part of our past; it defines our present and our future.

The moments when the United Kingdom has come together to applaud its care and essential workers will be remembered as an expression of our national spirit; and its symbol will be the rainbows drawn by children.

Across the Commonwealth and around the world, we have seen heart-warming stories of people coming together to help others, be it through delivering food parcels and medicines, checking on neighbors, or converting businesses to help the relief effort.

And though self-isolating may at times be hard, many people of all faiths, and of none, are discovering that it presents an opportunity to slow down, pause and reflect, in prayer or meditation.

It reminds me of the very first broadcast I made, in 1940, helped by my sister. We, as children, spoke from here at Windsor to children who had been evacuated from their homes and sent away for their own safety.

Today, once again, many will feel a painful sense of separation from their loved ones.

But now, as then, we know, deep down, that it is the right thing to do.

While we have faced challenges before, this one is different. This time we join with all nations across the globe in a common endeavor, using the great advances of science and our instinctive compassion to heal.

We will succeed — and that success will belong to every one of us.

We should take comfort that while we may have more still to endure, better days will return: We will be with our friends again; we will be with our families again; we will meet again.

But for now, I send my thanks and warmest good wishes to you all.

五、补充阅读

1）Jones, R. (1998). *Conference Interpreting Explained*. Manchester: St. Jerome Publishing.

2）Zhong, W. (2003). Memory training in interpreting. *Translation Journal*, 7(3), 1-9.

3）王斌华. 口译：理论·技巧·实践 [M]. 武汉：武汉大学出版社，2006.

第**4**章 ▶ 短期记忆-2

一、技能解说

1）有许多记忆方法可以帮助记忆，如信息视觉化、顺时记忆、空间记忆、树状记忆、反差记忆等。

2）口译记忆是对源语意义的记忆，理解性记忆是口译记忆的主要手段。认知科学认为，理解是对意义的心智感应能力，"理解力"在认知心理学中也称为"认知能力"。而口译的理解有其本身的特征。这些特征是：一、重听觉（即视觉）感应；二、重关联能力；三、重逻辑推理；四、重整体把握及意义—意向整合（刘宓庆，2004，p. 141）。

3）形象记忆是促进记忆的有效手段。

- ✓ 形象的建立可以在口译中帮助减轻记忆负担，增强叙述类讲话复述的连贯性。
- ✓ 如果记忆的东西思路清晰，表达的时候就不会出现"语无伦次"。表达的内容不完全是大脑中呈现的形象，要根据原讲话的内容，依托形象记忆尽可能回忆相关的内容，从而准确表达信息意义（刘和平，2009，p. 23-24）。

4）注意是记忆的前提，理解是记忆的条件，意义的把握是记忆的关键；记忆不可能与原型相等、等同、对等；记忆受制于心理压力，心理压力越大，记忆效果越差，翻译效果越不好。

5）现在可以开始学习用笔记进行数字口译。

- ✓ 英汉数字口译常用加点划杠法。英文听到thousand、million、billion和trillion打逗号，逗号之间含三位数字。记下数字之后，从右到左每四位数字前划一个长斜杠，每个斜杠从右到左依次读为"万""亿""万亿/兆"，其他数字正常读出即可。
- ✓ 该练习应每周坚持，直到笔记阶段结束，每次练习一个点，如第一周练thousand，第二周练million，第三周练billion，第四周练trillion，第五周可以加单位，如square meter、hour、foot等。每周练习都在前一周练习基础之上完成，可以10个同类型数字为一组做小组练习，一人先快速用英文读出一组数字，同伴做口译练习，然后交换角色。

二、训练方法

- ● 记忆方法练习
  - ✓ 与同伴一起练习，一个人讲一则童年故事（时间顺序）或者介绍一栋建筑（空间顺序）；另一人听后复述，在保证关键信息正确、完整的前提下，尽量回忆更多的细节。

- 预测练习
  - ✔ 根据文章标题，猜测本篇可能要讲什么，有哪些主要论点和分论点（main ideas and sub-ideas），以及可能怎么讲（possible connections of the ideas）。
  - ✔ 与同学交流，进行头脑风暴，写下可能涉及的关键英文词汇。
  - ✔ 然后进行听后复述。
- 小组数字练习
  - ✔ 在小组内练习，先从含thousand的数字开始，每人列10个数字，请对方译成中文。掌握之后，列10个含million的数字，练习方法同前。掌握之后，再逐渐增加难度练习含billion和trillion的数字。
  - ✔ 总结译错的数字并分析原因。
- 特定材料练习：论述类讲话
  - ✔ 边听边分析边记忆，尤其要把相关的数字一起记住。
  - ✔ 如果数字和信息的记忆发生冲突，信息优先。

三、练习案例点评

─────────────────────── 案例1 ───────────────────────

源　语： Earlier on in today's lecture, I mentioned the importance of hand gestures and said that I'd touch on some of these, pardon the pun! Hand gestures are, of course, often culturally bound and can vary from group to group. But there are a few of them which, if not universal, are very common indeed around the world. I'd like to focus on the history of four gestures in particular: the salute, the thumbs-up, the high five, and the handshake.

The salute, a gesture most associated with the military, may have originated in the 18th century. The Grenadier Guards, one of the oldest regiments of the British Army, used helmets in the form of cones. These were held in place by chinstraps. It was difficult to raise your helmet when greeting someone, so the soldiers simply touched their head with one short movement of the hand before quickly putting it back down again at their side.

学生复述： I talked about the importance of hand, hand, hand gestures. Emm … Emm, now I want to talk about four of them. They are often related to culture. Emm, it is different in different places. Emm, some of them are universal. So I would like to focus on the history of four gestures: salute, thumbs up, high five and, and, and handshake. Salute is a gesture that is used by the British army, the, the, the Grenadier Guards in the military. It is easy for the soldiers to touch the helmet, then put down their hands quickly. So this is how this gesture came into place.

📋 点评

1）大意出来了，比较完整。

2）复述中有语法问题，it is different in different places中it指的是手势，前一句用they指代，这一句也应该用复数。

3）敬礼的历史细节复述得不太完整，但针对Grenadier Guards这个英国军队术语，采取了重复原音的方法，是比较好的应对策略。

4）这位同学有较多的自我重复，句首的填充词比较多。如果听的时候逻辑分析比较清楚，适当采取图像或形象记忆等方法，短期记忆就会比较清晰，就不容易出现过多的自我修正和填充词。

教师评分：83。

案例2

源　　语： America's national road system makes it possible to drive coast to coast. From the Atlantic Ocean in the east to the Pacific Ocean in the west is a distance of more than 4,000 kilometers. Or you could drive more than 2,000 kilometers and go from the Canadian border south to the Mexican border.

You can drive these distances on wide, safe roads that have no traffic signals and no stop signs. In fact, if you did not have to stop for gasoline or sleep, you could drive almost anywhere in the United States without stopping at all. This is possible because of the Interstate Highway System. The system has almost 70,000 kilometers of roads. It crosses more than 55,000 bridges, and can be found in 49 of America's 50 states.

学生复述： … In America, you can … emm, drive coast to coast. You can also drive emm, from the east … east to the west … west with more than 4,000 kilometers, and from the south to the north with more than 2,000 kilometers. You can drive on the safe road, because there are no traffic signs, signals, and stop signs. Actually, you can drive to almost anywhere in America due to the Interstate Highway System.

📋 点评

1）这段复述的主要问题包括：开口时不顺畅；丢失了很多信息；数字记忆差；语言组织不流畅，句式单一，有语言错误；复述语速慢，自我修正多。

2）第一个信息点的描述和表达不完整。利用空间记忆的方法，在脑海中构建美国地图的形象，可以更好地记住从东到西两个大洋之间约4,000千米，从北到南两个邻国之间约2,000千米。

3）描绘完空间，第二个信息点处，可以用关键词法概括大意，比如依次记为：两个no、为两件事停车、一直开。

4）结尾的数字没有复述出来。每个信息点都需要边听边分析，再选择恰当的策略来记忆，如先记关键词、最后记数字；长的专有名词the Interstate Highway System 用缩略词法记为IHS。表达的时候，把脑子里的内容用自己的语言加上记住的关键词，按记忆顺序说出来。

教师评分：65。

四、篇章练习

生词表

英文	中文
Grenadier Guards	掷弹兵近卫团（英国皇家御林军，英国近卫步兵第一团）
chinstrap	（系于颏下固定头盔等的）帽带
Colosseum	罗马斗兽场，罗马大角斗场，罗马圆形竞技场
Los Angeles Dodgers	洛杉矶道奇队（美国棒球队）
Louisville Cardinals	路易斯维尔红雀队（美国篮球队）
Acropolis Museum	雅典卫城博物馆
Hera	女神赫拉（古希腊神话中的第三代天后，婚姻与生育女神，奥林匹斯十二主神之一）
Athena	女神雅典娜（古希腊神话中智慧女神，雅典城的保护神，奥林匹斯十二主神之一）
curtsey	行屈膝礼
stray	偏离
Dwight Eisenhower	德怀特·艾森豪威尔（第34任美国总统）
the act of Congress	国会法案

（待续）

（续表）

英文	中文
Interstate Highway System	（美国）州际公路系统
Nashville	纳什维尔（美国田纳西州首府）
the Natchez Trace	纳切兹小径（美国早期道路）
wagon	四轮的运货马车
Saint Louis	圣路易斯（美国港口城市）
Times Square	时代广场，纽约时报广场
memoir	回忆录，自传
binge-watch	一次性看完（常指追剧）
counterintuitive	违反直觉的，有悖常理的
the Department of Motor Vehicles, DMV	机动车管理局（美国地方政府机构，职能类似我国车辆管理所）
doorstopper	厚重的大部头书籍
CrossFit	混合健身（综合了田径、体操、举重等许多动作进行无间歇练习）
triceps	三头肌
acronym	首字母缩略词
resentfully	充满愤恨地
recap	扼要重述

1）History of hand gestures

练习说明：

1. This is a talk about the history of some hand gestures. Brainstorm before listening: Can you guess what might be covered in this talk? Do you know something about the meanings and history of hand gestures? What kind of logical framework might be used in the talk, vertical or horizontal? Why?

2. The talk is divided into four segments. Retell the main idea of each segment at the stop signal and record your retelling.

3. After retelling,

   1) review your recording for quality: Did you get the correct message? Does your retelling contain any language fillers, pauses longer than three seconds, or disorganized information? If so, please try again to address the problems.

   2) think about the following questions:

      • Did you hear the background music when listening? Did it help you better understand the talk or distract you instead? Why? How did you cope with it?

- What is the logic flow of this talk?

Earlier on in today's lecture, I mentioned the importance of hand gestures and said that I'd touch on some of these, pardon the pun! Hand gestures are, of course, often culturally bound and can vary from group to group. But there are a few of them which, if not universal, are very common indeed around the world. I'd like to focus on the history of four gestures in particular: the salute, the thumbs-up, the high five, and the handshake.

The salute, a gesture most associated with the military, may have originated in the 18th century. The Grenadier Guards, one of the oldest regiments of the British Army, used helmets in the form of cones. These were held in place by chinstraps. It was difficult to raise your helmet when greeting someone, so the soldiers simply touched their head with one short movement of the hand before quickly putting it back down again at their side.

The thumbs-up gesture apparently goes back a lot further. It's widely believed that this gesture goes back to Roman times when gladiators fought in front of the emperor and eager crowds in the Colosseum. The fallen gladiator's fate was decided by the audience. If they felt he had fought well, they showed their approval with a thumbs-up gesture. The emperor would then confirm this and thereby would spare the gladiator's life. If the crowd gave a thumbs down, on the other hand, that meant execution.

However, there are no reliable historical references to thumbs going either up or down in the Colosseum. It may be that if the crowd wanted to spare the gladiator's life, then they would actually cover up their thumb and keep it hidden. They would only extend their hand and thumb if they wanted the gladiator killed. This actually makes more sense, as the emperor could much more easily see what the crowd was indicating when looking out over a huge arena.

The high-five hand gesture is almost universally used as a greeting or celebration. Two U.S. sports teams lay claim to inventing the high five: the Los Angeles Dodgers in 1977 or the Louisville Cardinals in 1978. It's quite likely that it was neither, and the gesture might have a much earlier origin again. It is very similar to a 1920s Jazz Age gesture known as the "low five," or "giving skin." This gesture involved people slapping each other's lower hands, also in celebration. There are, in fact, numerous references to the low five in films of the era. Perhaps the high five is just an evolution of that gesture.

The final gesture I'm going to mention today is the handshake. It dates back as a greeting at least as far as Ancient Greece. In the Acropolis Museum in Athens, the base of one of the columns shows goddess Hera shaking hands with Athena, the goddess of wisdom and courage. It's thought that shaking hands, rather than bowing or curtseying, showed both parties as equals. In 17th-century marriage portraits in Europe, we find many examples of handshakes between husband and wife. Now, of course, the handshake has a multitude of uses: meeting, greeting, parting, offering congratulations, expressing gratitude, or completing an agreement. In sports or other competitive activities, it is also done as a sign of good sportsmanship. In this way, the gesture has not strayed from its original meaning to convey trust, respect, and equality.

2）American highways

练习说明：

1. This is a talk titled "Going the Distance, Coast to Coast and Border to Border, on America's Highways." It is divided into 10 segments. Retell at each stop signal and record.
2. After retelling,
   1) review your recording for language quality: Did you get the correct message? Does your retelling contain any language fillers, pauses longer than three seconds, or disorganized information? If so, try again and address the problems.
   2) think about the following questions: What is the main idea of this talk? What are the sub-ideas? How did you link these ideas and memorize them? Did you find techniques like visualization or categorization effective? Share your memory techniques with your peers.

On June 29, 1956, President Dwight Eisenhower signed a public works bill. The act of Congress provided federal aid to build the Interstate Highway System.

America's national road system makes it possible to drive coast to coast. From the Atlantic Ocean in the east to the Pacific Ocean in the west is a distance of more than 4,000 kilometers. Or you could drive more than 2,000 kilometers and go from the Canadian border south to the Mexican border.

You can drive these distances on wide, safe roads that have no traffic signals and no stop signs. In fact, if you did not have to stop for gasoline or sleep, you could drive almost anywhere in the United States without stopping at all. This is possible because of the Interstate Highway System. This system has almost 70,000 kilometers of roads. It crosses more than 55,000 bridges and can be found in 49 of America's 50 states.

The Interstate Highway System is usually two roads, one in each direction, separated by an area that is planted with grass and trees. Each road holds two lines of cars that can travel at speeds between 100 and 120 kilometers an hour. The Interstate Highway System is only a small part of the huge system of roads in the United States.

To understand the Interstate Highway System, it is helpful to understand the history of roads. Roads in most countries were first built to permit armies to travel from one part of the country to another to fight against an invader.

The ancient Romans built roads over most of Europe to permit their armies to move quickly from one place to another. People who traded goods began using these roads for business. Good roads helped them to move their goods faster from one area to another.

No roads existed when early settlers arrived in the area of North America that would become the United States. Most settlers built their homes near the ocean or along major rivers. This made transportation easy. A few early roads were built near some cities. Travel on land was often difficult because there was no road system in most areas.

In 1785, farmers in the Ohio River Valley used rivers to take cut trees to the southern city of New Orleans. It was easier to walk or ride a horse home than to try to go by boat up the river.

One of the first roads was built to help these farmers return home after they sold their wood. It began as nothing more than a path used by Native Americans. American soldiers helped make this path into an early road. The new road extended from the city of Nashville in Tennessee to the city of Natchez in the southern state of Mississippi. It was called the Natchez Trace.

You can still follow about 700 kilometers of the Natchez Trace. Today, the road is a beautiful National Park. It takes the traveler through forests that look much the same as they did 200 years ago. You can still see a few of the buildings in which early travelers slept overnight.

The Natchez Trace was called a road. Yet it was not what we understand a road to be. It was just a cleared path through the forest. It was used by people walking, or riding a horse, or in a wagon pulled by horses.

In 1806, President Thomas Jefferson signed legislation that approved money for building a road to make it easier to travel west. Work began on the first part of the road in Cumberland in the eastern state of Maryland. When finished, the road reached all the way to the city of Saint Louis in what was to become the middle-western state of Missouri. It was named the National Road.

The National Road was similar to the Natchez Trace. It followed a path made by American

Indians. Work began in 1811. It was not finished until about 1833. The National Road was used by thousands of people who moved toward the west. These people paid money to use the road. This money was used to repair the road.

Now, the old National Road is part of United States Highway 40. By the 1920s, Highway 40 stretched from the Atlantic Ocean to the Pacific Ocean. You can still see signs that say "National Road" along the side of parts of it. Several statues were placed along this road to honor the women who moved west over the National Road in the 1800s.

In 1900, it still was difficult to travel by road. Nothing extended from the eastern United States to the extreme western part of the country.

Several people wanted to see a road built all the way across the country. Carl Fisher was a man who had ideas and knew how to act on them. Mr. Fisher built the famous Indianapolis Motor Speedway where car races still take place.

In 1912, Carl Fisher began working on his idea to build a coast-to-coast highway using crushed rocks. He called this dream the Coast-to-Coast Rock Highway.

Carl Fisher asked many people to give money for the project. One of these men was Henry Joy, the president of the Packard Motor Car Company. Mr. Joy agreed, but suggested another name for the highway. He said the road should be named after President Abraham Lincoln. He said it should be called the Lincoln Highway.

Everyone involved with the project agreed to the new name. The Lincoln Highway began in the east in New York City's famous Times Square. It ended in the west in Lincoln Park in San Francisco, California. The Lincoln Highway was completed in the 1930s.

Later, the federal government decided to assign each highway in the country its own number. Numbers were easier to remember than names. The Lincoln Highway became Highway 30 for most of its length.

Today, you can still follow much of the Lincoln Highway. It passes through small towns and large cities. This makes it a slow but interesting way to travel. Highway 30 still begins in New York and ends near San Francisco. And it is still remembered as the first coast-to-coast highway.

In 1919, a young Army officer named Dwight Eisenhower took part in the first crossing of the United States by Army vehicles. The vehicles left Washington, D.C. and drove to San Francisco. It was not a good trip. The vehicles had problems with thick mud, ice, and mechanical difficulties.

It took the American Army vehicles 62 days to reach San Francisco.

Dwight Eisenhower believed the United States needed a highway that would aid in the defense of the country. He believed the nation needed a road system that would permit military vehicles to travel quickly from one coast to the other.

In 1956, Dwight Eisenhower was president of the United States. He signed the legislation that created the federal Interstate Highway System. Work was begun almost immediately.

Building such an interstate highway system was a major task. Many problems had to be solved. The highway passed through different areas that were wetlands, mountains and deserts. It was very difficult to build the system. Yet lessons learned while building it influenced the building of highways around the world. Today, the interstate system links every major city in the United States. It also links the United States with Canada and Mexico.

The Interstate Highway System has been an important part of the nation's economic growth during the past 40 years. Experts believe that trucks using the system carry about 75 percent of all products that are sold. Jobs and new businesses have been created near the busy interstate highways all across the United States. These include hotels, motels, eating places, gasoline stations and shopping centers.

The highway system has made it possible for people to work in a city and live outside it. And it has made it possible for people to travel easily and quickly from one part of the country to another.

The United States government renamed the Interstate Highway System at the end of the 20th century. Large signs now can be seen along the side of the highway that say Eisenhower Interstate System.

3）How to read books

练习说明:
1. This is a public radio podcast about how to read books. It is divided into eight segments. Retell at each stop signal and record.
2. After retelling, review your recording for language quality and think about the following questions:
   1) Did you use the skills of question & answer, visualization, or association to help you memorize the ideas and sub-ideas? What other memory techniques did you use?
   2) How did you memorize numbers?

Hostess: Today, we're talking about how to read more. And you know what? I'm going to start this episode with a confession. I read a lot of articles and magazines and nonfiction journalism, but I have been halfway through Michelle Obama's memoir, *Becoming*, for upwards of six months. There are also about seven books on my nightstand that I have not read. And actually, there's an entire pile of books in the corner of one room that used to be on my nightstand until they felt too judgmental of me, and I had to move them.

I know that a pile of unread books seems like a bad look, but I really do love reading. As an only child growing up, I never left the house without a book. There was an entire genre of kid photo of me at family gatherings where I'm, like, up a tree with a book instead of at the table with everybody else, you know?

But I don't know. There are just so many shows to binge-watch. And I feel like my life is full of people and things that need my attention. And then there's that other thing that often gets our attention.

(Soundbite of cellphone vibrating) Oops, going to put that on airplane mode. It feels like I sit down to read a book, and then, all of a sudden, it's two hours later and I'm three months back into an Instagram account for cats with their mouth open. Side note, that account exists, and it is fantastic. Anyway, I know I'm not alone.

Hostess: What do you personally do as a "Book Queen"?

Neary: Well — "Book Queen."

Hostess: Yes. That's your job title, isn't it, "Queen of books"?

Neary: All right. I'm going to put that down, "Book Queen." I like that. Yes. One always wants to be a queen of something.

Hostess: Well, look at that … Your very own "queendom."

Hostess: That's Lynn Neary, who has been covering books for a decade, so she's got, like, royalty status.

Neary: People always say, how many books have you read this month? You know, how many books do you read for your job? And I never really want to sort of reveal that because I feel like that's my own private, secret, little number.

Hostess: Lynn might be able to build herself an entire house out of the books that she reads for her job. But she says that she's actually not a speed-reader. But she also says that that's OK and that we should all just take it easy on ourselves when it comes to the pace that we read at.

Neary: I always feel like I probably should be a faster reader than I am to do this job. But I just think people should settle down about that. Read at your own pace. Read it the way you're comfortable reading. Read the way you like to read because it should be something that's pleasurable.

Hostess: Lynn also has the same struggle that many of us do — that transfixing pull of, literally, all other forms of entertainment.

Neary: I think the idea of binge-watching TV is one of the biggest competitions for me with reading because as a reader and as somebody who loves stories and narratives, I think … there's such great television out there right now. And it's just easier for me to watch television than it is to read a book.

Hostess: Lynn has some expert advice for getting more reading done. I know I'm not the only one with books on my nightstand. And sometimes, I don't get through more than a few pages before falling asleep if I do it at night. Her advice is our first takeaway — read in the morning.

Neary: I don't know exactly when this began. But at a certain point within the last, let's say, 10 years since I started covering books, I started waking up earlier than I used to. And I'd be awake. And I really didn't want to be awake. You know, it was like 6:00 or 6:30 or something. And I'd think, this is too early. I don't want to get out of bed right now. And so I began reading. And I think I had this idea that maybe I would read myself back to sleep if I picked up a book. And what I discovered was I was wide awake. And it was a really good time to read.

Hostess: Obviously, this might not work for you depending on where you're at in your life or what time your alarm goes off. But it feels, like, counterintuitive, which I think might mean that it's a brilliant idea.

Hostess: Another expert we spoke to, Kevin Nguyen, he's been working in books for many, many years and reads on average 100 books a year. He has a great piece that he wrote last year called "How to read a whole book every week." Kevin is also a big morning reader. He says the key is if you want to read more, you have to make it really, really easy.

Nguyen: The hardest part about reading a book is just, like, opening the book.
Hostess: Right.
Nguyen: I think (for) a lot of people, when they sit down and they read, it's not hard to get lost in it. It's not hard to just actually read the book. It's just easy to be distracted by your phone and any other number of things going on in your life. So I think part of it is, you

know, we have this imagination of like, "oh, reading time is, like, this luxurious thing." I'm in my armchair sipping Scotch. Or I'm, you know, about to go to bed, you know? And I think it's … you have to make it a more regular habit than that because if you just wait for all those times when you're drinking Scotch … Hopefully, you don't drink that much Scotch. I hope you read more than you drink Scotch. But, yeah, if you wait for all those moments, you're never going to finish a book.

Hostess: I think he's so right about this. I mean, I respect Michelle Obama so much. And in my head, I've been thinking that in order to give her words the attention they deserve, I've got to have, like, an uninterrupted span of seven hours and my perfect mug of tea and the perfect light and my fuzziest socks.

But you know what? Michelle … I'm going to call her Michelle. Michelle will never know if I read her book on my phone while I'm standing on the subway platform avoiding my nemesis, a subway busker who plays "Free Fallin'" by Tom Petty every single morning. Michelle Obama is never going to know. OK. So this is our second takeaway — read when you can wherever you are, especially if you're commuting.

Nguyen: It's a built-in thing in your day. You're driving to work. It's audiobook time. You get on the subway. It's time to, like, open the book. I'm not going to play video games on my phone or listen to a podcast. It's really easy to have that kind of discipline because it's sort of like a sequestered part of your day where you decide "I'm doing this thing at this time." Another thing I like about reading on your phone is it's always with you. So, like, when you're in line at, like, a café and you just know it's going to be, like, a five-minute wait, like, that's five minutes you can read right there.

Hostess: Yeah.

Nguyen: And those minutes add up a lot.

Hostess: Having a book with you for all those little in-betweeny [in-between] moments of your day is so smart, right? Like, when you're waiting for the bus or in any kind of line, that's when you read. Audiobooks are also a really great way to do this, too, because that means that — boom — the car is now fair game for getting some reading time. When Kevin showed up for our interview, he had two paper books in his bag, plus several that he was reading on his phone.

And while we're talking about phones, this could be a really smart way for you to rethink your relationship to your phone, you know? Like, if you're getting through a few more pages of Michelle Obama instead of scrolling through the really dismal news coverage — I don't know — that sounds like a win to me.

Hostess: Here's takeaway number three: Match the kind of book that you're reading to the amount of time that you have.

Nguyen: I'm usually reading a couple novels at a time, a nonfiction book, and then maybe a comic book …

Hostess: I see.

Nguyen: … Because they just feel so different. And then, like, when I found myself with, like, you know, 20 to 40 minutes on a commute — because that's the span of the subway commute — it could be 20 minutes or 40 minutes.

Hostess: Yeah, (you) never know.

Nguyen: That was enough time for me to get through a bit of the novel.

Hostess: Because books have different textures and they demand different kinds of attention from your little brain, it's smart to dip your eyes into something lighter when you're at the DMV, for example. I mean, the DMV is dark enough on its own. So then you can save that historical doorstopper for when you're in the right place to really take it in.

There's another thing that's beneficial to reading multiple books at multiple speeds at the same time, too. It can give you a sense of achievement, which is our next takeaway — track your reading. Some people keep track of how many pages they've read in their books, but Kevin just has a little note in his phone with all of the books that he's completed.

Nguyen: And that's part of the feeling of accomplishment and momentum. It's funny how, like, quantifying these things can actually be pretty encouraging. I know, like, if you do CrossFit, you know, like, you write down your exercise and your times that day, which sounds very corny, but there's no reason that you can't keep track of that.

Hostess: Look, I have never done CrossFit, but I have watched my friends' triceps appear before my very eyes as they posted all these weird acronyms and stuff on Instagram. And stay with me here — reading is like CrossFit for your brain on some level, right? I like to think of tracking your reading as a thing that I sometimes do when I'm making a to-do list — right? — where I, like, write down a few things that maybe I've already done. Or maybe they're, like, really simple things — just so that I can cross them off and feel this, like, rush of accomplishment. Kevin just uses the notes app on his phone. But some people also use sites to track what they've been reading. And if you want, you can also track your reading by posting about it on social media.

Nguyen: I see a lot of people keep track of that stuff on Instagram and will tweet about it. I think it's a great idea, you know, because taking a photo of a book and putting it on

Instagram is, like, a good way to keep track of your goal and also, like, tell people you read a book. Then people know you read it and maybe want to talk to you about it. They've also read it. And then what's always funny is, like, you sort of see, like, midway through the year, the books start to get, like, a little skinnier. Suddenly, there's, like, a poetry collection in there. But I think that's totally fine.

Hostess: Both Kevin and Lynn told me that it's important to accept that not every book is going to be the one that grabs you. When you start a book, sometimes, it feels like this promise that you're making to yourself. But I think it's important to say here that you have to be able to let it go if you can't push through a book. You don't have to like every book.

Nguyen: One challenging thing I think about goals — especially, like, an every-week goal — it's like, you're just going to go a week where you didn't finish a book. Like, maybe you were on vacation, or work was really tough. That's OK. It's OK to fall off the wagon and just push yourself to, like, make up that week.

Hostess: Here's the thing that really appeals to me about tracking my reading. Like those folks who, all of a sudden, are posting their poetry collection, I feel an incredible rush of accomplishment when I finish a book quickly. And if I'm following Kevin's example and reading lots of different books at the same time, I'll feel good with some momentum from speeding through one book so that I don't get caught in my current situation where there's just one lonely book sitting there half-read and then a whole pile of other ones looking at me resentfully.

Hostess: OK, readers, listeners — well, whatever you are — let's recap everything that we talked about on this episode so that you can turn this podcast off and get fired up on some reading, OK? First, don't be afraid to read first thing in the morning before your whole day happens to you. Second, read in the in-betweeny [in-between] moments, especially when you're already trapped somewhere or commuting. Third, match the book you're reading to the amount of time that you have. And finally, track your reading so that you can feel like you're really getting somewhere.

五、补充阅读

1）刘宓庆. 口笔译理论研究 [M]. 北京：中国对外翻译出版公司，2004.

2）刘和平. 法语口译教程 [M]. 上海：上海外语教育出版社，2009.

第5章 ▶ 应对策略

一、技能解说

1）口译记忆针对的是信息，而不是源语讲话的具体用词。如果记忆只停留在源语的字词表层，未能对信息进行逻辑分析等深加工，那么信息遗忘的概率则相对较高。听完后如果只记住了一些细节，对信息的组织和结构却很模糊，不仅很难复述出整段信息大意，且容易出现表达不流畅、大段遗忘甚至瞎编乱说等情况，应尽量避免。

2）讲话者语速太快、口音太重，讲话内容信息太密集，译者太紧张导致一个词一个句子没听见就慌了……听时出现这些状况，应当如何应对？

- ✓ 首先尽量保持冷静，至少做到在声音、表情上不显露。
- ✓ 说出意思或大概意思，忽略没听懂的词，根据上下文合理猜测大意，有时可以用重复的方式补缺。
- ✓ 条件允许的话，可以向讲话者就某个具体句子或意思提问。

3）接受一个事实：口译本身就是"危机管理"（crisis management）。译前准备、自信的心态、语言水平和口译技巧等都可能影响应对策略。

二、训练方法

- 养成良好习惯。
  - ✓ 在练习复述时，养成开口就一定要说完一整句的习惯，尽量避免话说半句后改口。
  - ✓ 察觉自己要说"嗯""啊"的时候立刻闭嘴，想好了要说什么再开口，逐渐养成习惯。
- 增加"刻意练习"。
  - ✓ 练习前一定要明确1~2个练习目标，并在练习过程中严格执行。
  - ✓ 练完一定要寻求同伴或教师的反馈。
- 继续进行记忆训练，增强短期记忆能力。
  - ✓ 可选用超市购物清单、童年故事、最记忆深刻的一件事等内容进行复述练习。

三、练习案例点评

案例1

源　　语： So for example, *The Cat in the Hat Comes Back*, a book that I'm sure we all often return to, like *Moby Dick*. One phrase in it is, "Do you know where I found him? Do you know where he was? He was eating cake in the tub. Yes he was!" Fine. Now, (if) you learn that in Mandarin Chinese, then you have to master, "You can know, I did where him find? He was tub inside gorging cake. No mistake gorging chewing!" That just feels good. Imagine being able to do that for years and years at a time.

Or, have you ever learned any Cambodian? Me either, but if I did, I would get to roll around in my mouth not some baker's dozen of vowels like English has, but a good 30 different vowels scooching and oozing around in the Cambodian mouth like bees in a hive. That is what a language can get you.

学生复述： For example, there is a book about cat in hats, which has a famous line like this: "Do you know where I found him? He was in the tub, eating a cake." But if you learn … have learned Mandarin Chinese, the word order turns out to be totally different. So that makes the language very fun … language learning very fun. Another example is that if you speak in Cambodian, then … it is totally different from English because in Cambodia there are 30 vowels. You have to speak them in your mouth, so busy like bees in a hive. This is so much fun.

> 📋 **点评**

1）复述大意比较完整。原句大意就是两个例子，复述的难点在于学生不熟悉讲话者提到的书，而且文字细节没法全部原样复述出来。

2）You can know, I did where him find? He was tub inside gorging cake. No mistake gorging chewing! 这几句英文是按中文语序排列的，没有逻辑或规律，很难复述。但可以根据自己学习外语时的类似感受，把理解的意思用英文再说出来即可。

3）复述中有不少语言错误，如has a famous line、Mandarin in Chinese、speak in Cambodian等表达不妥；it is totally different from English应该是it is totally different from speaking English。复述中还有许多自我修正。要养成边说边监听自己语言输出质量的习惯，尽量开口就不出错。

教师评分：85。

源　语：Another value which has been revived is the value in Chinese "礼." In English, we can translate it as "ritual propriety." The idea is that we can use laws to regulate people to stop them from doing bad things. But if we really want to have a kind of harmonious society, that comes to informal mechanisms, like rituals that generate a sense of community. So, this is one reason why the idea of ritual propriety has been revived in different spheres of social and even political life in China.

Another value that's been revived a lot is filial piety, "孝," which we can also translate as reverence for elderly members of the family and ancestors. So one of the festivals that has been revived in China is called the Qingming Festival, the ancestor worship festival. And this is sort of thing that evolved from the bottom. Literally, hundreds of millions of ordinary Chinese people took the day off on that particular day to worship their ancestors. And eventually, the government said, "Well, fine, let's just make it into a national holiday." So, a lot of this revival comes from the bottom up, not just from the top.

学生复述：So another reason for the revival of Confucianism is "礼," which is called ritual propriety. And you can say that a law, or laws are, emm, designed to regulate people, but we also need some mechanisms that can regulate people from within instead of from without. And "礼" actually plays a role, emm, in doing so. And still another value for the revival of Confucianism is called "孝," which is filial piety, emm, filial piety. And this is a kind of respect of the order in the social or political spheres and mainly, it is the worship of people or the respect to people who are older than you or something else. For example, in China, in … at the Qingming Festival, er, which is the ancestor worship festival, people often get together to worship their ancestors. And the government sees that and says, "Well, let's make it … make it a national holiday." And, so this also shows that all these changes are from, um, down to above.

点评

1）复述的准确性和完整性都比较高，是听懂和分析记忆之后把理解的意思用英文陈述出来，大意和细节都完整。

2）复述中有一些小的自我重复和填充词，以及一些语言不当，如：who are older than you or something else 这个表达突然转为第二人称，all these changes are from, um, down to above 表达欠妥、不够明确，等等。

教师评分：90。

四、篇章练习

生词表

英文	中文
acid trip	迷幻之旅
enticing	诱人的，有吸引力的，迷人的
fraught	令人担心的，令人焦虑的
flutter	（心）扑通扑通地跳
imbibe	吸收，接纳
Jesus of Montreal	《蒙特利尔的耶稣》（加拿大法语电影）
husk	外壳，皮，荚
scrim curtain	网纱帘幕（舞台用，单向透光）
Amharic	阿姆哈拉语（埃塞俄比亚官方语言）
witch hazel	金缕梅酊剂（用于治疗皮肤创伤）
The Cat in the Hat Comes Back	《戴帽子的猫回来了》（经典儿童故事）
Moby Dick	《白鲸》（19世纪美国小说家赫尔曼·梅尔维尔著长篇小说）
scooch	（坐着或蹲着时）往旁边挪一下位置
ooze	渗出，冒出，分泌出
cut one's teeth on	从…中获得初步经验
bourbon	波旁威士忌
Dilbert	呆伯特（漫画家斯科特·亚当斯所著连环漫画）
antidepressant	抗抑郁药
adolescents	青少年
Food and Drug Administration, FDA	美国食品药品监督管理局
American Psychiatric Association	美国精神医学会
cryptic	神秘的，晦涩的，隐晦的
seniority	年长，资历，辈分
demonization	妖魔化，恶魔化
denounce	谴责
otherworldly	超凡脱俗的，超脱尘世的

1）Four reasons to learn a new language

练习说明：

1. This is a talk about why one should learn a new language. Brainstorm before listening: Can you come up with some reasons for learning a new language? If you were to give this talk, how would you organize it?

2. The talk contains specific language-related terms that might be challenging to understand or interpret, such as varied pronunciations of the same word in different languages, and books, movies, and apps which focus on foreign languages. How would you cope with them?

3. The talk is divided into nine segments. Retell at each stop signal and record your retelling.

4. After retelling, review your recording for language quality and answer the following questions:

   1) How did you manage to memorize each idea and sub-idea? Discuss different memory techniques with your peers.

   2) Reflecting upon your STM, how did you analyze what you have heard and understood? What messages did you miss and why?

The language I'm speaking right now is on its way to becoming the world's universal language, for better or for worse. Let's face it — it's the language of the Internet; it's the language of finance; it's the language of air traffic control, of popular music, diplomacy — English is everywhere.

Now, Mandarin Chinese is spoken by more people, but more Chinese people are learning English than English speakers are learning Chinese. Last I heard, there are two dozen universities in China right now teaching all in English.

And in addition to that, it's been predicted that at the end of the century almost all of the languages that exist now — there are about 6,000 — will no longer be spoken. There will only be some hundreds left. And on top of that, it's at the point where instant translation of live speech is not only possible, but it gets better every year.

The reason I'm reciting those things to you is ~~because~~ [that] I can tell that we're getting to the point where a question is going to start being asked, which is: Why should we learn foreign languages, other than if English happens to be foreign to one? Why bother to learn another one when it's getting to the point where almost everybody in the world will be able to communicate in one?

I think there are a lot of reasons, but I first want to address the one that you're probably most likely to have heard of, because actually it's more dangerous than you might think. And that is the idea that a language channels your thoughts, that the vocabulary and the grammar of different languages gives everybody a different kind of acid trip, so to speak. That is a marvelously enticing idea, but it's kind of fraught.

So it's not that it's untrue completely. So for example, in French and Spanish the word for "table" is, for some reason, marked as feminine. So, "*la table*," "*la mesa*," you just have to deal with it. It has been shown that if you are a speaker of one of those languages and you happen to be asked how you would imagine a table talking, then much more often than could possibly be an accident, a French or a Spanish speaker says that the table would talk with a high and feminine voice. So if you're French or Spanish, to you, a table is kind of a girl, as opposed to if you are an English speaker.

It's hard not to love data like that, and many people will tell you that that means that there's a worldview that you have if you speak one of those languages. But you have to watch out, because imagine if somebody put us under the microscope, the "us" being those of us who speak English natively. What is the worldview from English?

So for example, let's take an English speaker. Bono. He speaks English. I presume he has a worldview. Ms. Kardashian. And she is (an) English speaker, too. What worldview do those people have in common? What worldview is shaped through the English language that unites them? It's a highly fraught concept. And so gradual consensus is becoming that language can shape thought, but it tends to be in rather darling, obscure psychological flutters. It's not a matter of giving you a different pair of glasses on the world.

Now, if that's the case, then why learn languages? If it isn't going to change the way you think, what would the other reasons be? There are some. One of them is that if you want to imbibe a culture, if you want to drink it in, if you want to become part of it, then whether or not the language channels the culture — and that seems doubtful — if you want to imbibe the culture, you have to control to some degree the language that the culture happens to be conducted in. There's no other way.

There's an interesting illustration of this. I have to go slightly obscure, but really you should seek it out. There's a movie by the Canadian film director Denys Arcand — read out in English on the page, "Dennis Ar-cand," if you want to look him up. He did a film called *Jesus of Montreal*. And many of the characters are vibrant, funny, passionate, interesting French Canadian, French-speaking women. There's one scene closest to the end, where they have to take a friend to an anglophone hospital. In the hospital, they have to speak English. Now, they speak English but it's not their native language. They'd rather not speak English. And they speak it more slowly; they have accents; they're not idiomatic. Suddenly these characters that you've fallen in love with become husks of themselves; they're shadows of themselves.

To go into a culture and to only ever process people through that kind of scrim curtain is to never truly get the culture. And so to the extent that hundreds of languages will be left, one reason to learn them is because [that] they are tickets to being able to participate in the culture of the people who speak them, just by virtue of the fact that it is their code. So that's one reason.

Second reason: It's been shown that if you speak two languages, dementia is less likely to set in, and that you are probably a better multitasker. And these are factors that set in early, and so that ought to give you some sense of when to give junior or "*juniorette*" lessons in another language. Bilingualism is healthy.

And then, third — languages are just an awful lot of fun. Much more fun than we're often told. So for example, Arabic: "*Kataba*" he wrote. "*Yaktubu*" he writes. "*Uktub*" write, in the imperative. What do those things have in common? All those things have in common the consonants sitting in the middle like pillars. They stay still, and the vowels dance around the consonants. Who wouldn't want to roll that around in their mouths? You can get that from Hebrew. You can get that from Ethiopia's main language, Amharic. That's fun.

Or languages have different word orders. Learning how to speak with different word order is like driving on the different side of a street if you go to a certain country, or the feeling that you get when you put witch hazel around your eyes and you feel the tingle. A language can do that to you.

So for example, *The Cat in the Hat Comes Back*, a book that I'm sure we all often return to, like *Moby Dick*. One phrase in it is, "Do you know where I found him? Do you know where he was? He was eating cake in the tub. Yes he was!" Fine. Now, (if) you learn that in Mandarin Chinese, then you have to master, "You can know, I did where him find? He was tub inside gorging cake. No mistake gorging chewing!" That just feels good. Imagine being able to do that for years and years at a time.

Or, have you ever learned any Cambodian? Me either, but if I did, I would get to roll around in my mouth not some baker's dozen of vowels like English has, but a good 30 different vowels scooching and oozing around in the Cambodian mouth like bees in a hive. That is what a language can get you.

And more to the point, we live in an era when it's never been easier to teach yourself another language. It used to be that you had to go to a classroom, and there would be some diligent teacher — some genius teacher in there — but that person was only in there at certain times and you had to go then, and then was not most times. You had to go to class. If you didn't have that, you had something called a record. I cut my teeth on those. There was only ever so much data on a record, or a cassette, or even that antique object known as a CD. Other than that, you had books that didn't work. That's just the way it was.

Today you can ~~lay~~ [lie] down — lie on your living room floor, sipping bourbon, and teach yourself any language that you want to with wonderful sets such as Rosetta Stone. I highly recommend the lesser known Glossika as well. You can do it any time; therefore, you can do it more and better. You can give yourself your morning pleasures in various languages. I take some "*Dilbert*" in various languages every single morning; it can increase your skills. Couldn't have done it 20 years ago when the idea of having any language you wanted in your pocket, coming from your phone, would have sounded like science fiction to very sophisticated people.

So I highly recommend that you teach yourself languages other than the one that I'm speaking, because there's never been a better time to do it. It's an awful lot of fun. It won't change your mind, but it will most certainly blow your mind.

Thank you very much.

2）The antidepressant-suicide link

练习说明：

1. This is an excerpt of a news program about the link between suicide and antidepressants. It is reported that health officials were informed that antidepressants may elevate suicide risk in some patients.
2. The excerpt is divided into three segments. Retell at each stop signal and record your retelling.
3. After retelling,
   1) review your recording for language quality: Did you get the correct message of each segment? Does your retelling contain any language fillers, pauses longer than three seconds, or disorganized information? If so, try again and address the problems.
   2) think about the following questions:
      - What is the main idea of this talk? What are the sub-ideas? How did you link and memorize these main ideas and sub-ideas when interpreting?
      - How did you manage to memorize the proper names and numbers? Discuss with your peers why you missed, if any, some of the information points.

Hostess: This morning in Health Watch a very sticky issue for doctors who proscribe antidepressants. On Wednesday, government health officials heard arguments that those drugs actually raise the risk of suicide in some patients. And Dr. Emily Senay is here with details. Good morning, Emily.

Dr. Senay: Good morning!

Hostess: Where does this concern come from?

Dr. Senay: Right, well, we have to remember about nine percent of adults had (depression) (at) any given time during a year; eight percent of adolescents will have depression during a particular year. Now doctors have been treating patients for many years with antidepressants. The question has been, in some cases: Does that use of an antidepressant early on when they are first getting treatment increase the risk that the patient(s) might have suicidal thought or even commit suicide? That's been discussed, now, for several years. We know from previous studies that in children and adolescents, there appears to be an increased risk that they would have this suicidal thinking. What was new yesterday, was an analysis of new data looking at whether or not that might extend to other age groups.

Hostess: So, this new data said what?

Dr. Senay: This new data actually found that this risk does extend to people (aged) 25 and under. So, what the FDA advisory committee meeting wants to do then is (to) expand the warning to people who are under the age of 25. They were somewhat more likely in these studies to have the suicidal thinking. We have to point out here, though, that this risk is very, very small. Out of about 1,000 people, about four would have this increased risk of suicidal thinking.

Hostess: So, adding this warning label is a move in the right direction, right?

Dr. Senay: Well, what is currently on the antidepressant labels is the black box warning. That's the strongest warning label that the FDA puts out. The focus had been on children and adolescents. So, it's already there. They want to include now, this older age group. So that is what is the latest thinking here as this black box warning label has been out for quite some time.

Hostess: All right. So what do you do if you are under the age of 25, and you are battling depression and your doctor wants to put you on antidepressants? How do you know if it's gonna work for you or against you?

Dr. Senay: Well, the most … the important thing — and this was [is] what many doctors who treat patients and the American Psychiatric Association is [are] concerned about — is that people will see this black box warning label, though. Here the media attention that we give to it, and then, (they might) not seek treatment. In fact, they put out the statement yesterday on their website that exactly pointed this out, saying that the statistic ~~suggest~~ [suggests] that when the FDA considers mandating a black label, the subsequent media controversy and unjustified panic leave two millions of Americans not getting treatment. In fact, they pointed the fact that since 2004, there has been an increase in suicide. So their major concern is that this will scare parents away, (and) scare patients away from getting treated, for what is a pretty small problem. They did ~~loud~~ [appalled] the FDA advisory panel yesterday for suggesting or wanting the FDA to go ahead and add to the labels information about the risk of untreated depression. So they really want to see a more balanced approach, and that's the message for patients. Patients should still get treated absolutely. What everybody should know is that monitoring in the earliest phases of treatment is very very important.

Hostess: I know, Senay. Thank you so much!

Dr. Senay: OK.

- -

3）Revival of Confucianism in China

练习说明:

1. In this material, a sinologist talks about key values of Confucianism and the reasons for its revival in China in the past 30 years. Brainstorm on this topic before listening: What do you think the talk is going to be about? What are the key values that you know in Confucianism? Can you give some examples and discuss their significance? What might cause difficulties in understanding and memory when you retell the talk? And how can you cope with them?

2. The talk is divided into seven segments. Try to retell the message at the stop signal and record your retelling.

3. After retelling,
   1) review your retelling for language quality.
   2) think about the following questions:
      - Did you find memory skills and techniques helpful when memorizing the ideas and sub-ideas? Consider the skills of question & answer, visualization, and summarization. What other memory techniques did you use?
      - For details you failed to memorize, how did you cope with the information loss?

Welcome to China Talk. My name is Daniel Bell. Chinese name is Bei Danning. And I'm from Montreal, Canada, but I've spent about half of my life living and working in China. And during that time, I've come to love and appreciate Confucianism, contrary to my initial impressions of the tradition as a kind of boring and conservative and dead philosophy. The more I learn about Confucianism, the more I realize that it's very much a living and evolving philosophy.

Starting with Confucius himself. Confucius — again, there is a stereotype of him in the West as this boring and conservative teacher, who just says, pronounces cryptic words that his students blindly accept. But actually, it's very different. What he says is tailored individually to each student's needs and particularities. There's an assumption that everyone can improve, and the role of a teacher is to improve each student in his or her own way. That's why now in China, he's known as a teacher of teachers.

Now, the thing about Confucianism is that, it's very much a living philosophy, and (it) especially influences people in Shandong Province, which is a province of 100 million people. And people in Shandong tend to take great pride in their Confucian heritage. And it influences the way that people act in everyday life. If, for example, when there's a seating arrangement at a table, it's done according to seniority. But then eventually everybody is involved in the toasting and the eating, and it generates a strong sense of community and emotional bonding. So the hierarchies in Confucianism … They benefit those at the bottom end of the hierarchies. That's what makes them desirable in the modern world.

So I had learned a lot about Confucianism, and I was lucky enough to be offered a post ~~as~~ of dean at Shandong University, which is a leading university in Shandong Province. And I wrote a book about my experience, which is called *The Dean of Shandong*. And my aim in writing this book was both to honor my fellow students and teachers and administrators at Shandong University, and also frankly, I worry about the demonization of China in the West, for much of the reporting about China is entirely negative.

So in my book, I do discuss the problems, but I try to do so in a balanced way, and try to show that there's a lot of humanity and humor in everyday life, in academia, and even in politics that we should appreciate, rather than just blindly denounce. Now, some of the other values are involved. One of them is (what) we usually mistranslated as "harmony," in Chinese, "和谐的和" ("*he*" in the word "*he xie*"). Because in English, we don't distinguish between harmony typically, and conformity, especially when you talk about politics. Harmony sounds a little bit sinister, meaning that everybody thinks alike and has followed similar actions.

I remember watching the Beijing Olympics opening ceremony. And there was one character, this character "和" was chosen to represent Chinese culture. And I remember I was watching an American journalist, who said, "Look at that! All the soldiers are marching in the same way. That's pretty scary that everybody thinks and acts alike." But in Chinese, everybody knows this saying from the *Analects* of Confucius, "和而不同" ("harmony in diversity") ~~that~~ (where) we specifically distinguish between "harmony" and "同," which we can translate as "conformity" or "uniformity."

So the idea of "和" really involves respecting, in fact, loving diversity, appreciating diversity, but on a kind of foundation of peaceful order. So (it's like) some of the metaphors, including a soup: It's bland if it has one ingredient; but if it has many ingredients, then it's a delicious soup. Even in politics, if you have different views, it actually helps the country. This is the meaning of "和." So a better translation in English should be "harmony in diversity." That's really central to the Confucian ethic.

Now, you might ask: Why has Confucianism been revived? Because it was more or less dead for much of the 20th century in China, where the main tradition was a tradition of anti-traditionalism. But ~~since~~ 30 years ago, history has made a raging comeback in China. People take great pride in their historical heritage. And politically, the main tradition was Confucianism, and it had great influence.

Now, as mentioned, Confucianism is very diverse, and it has many different interpretations. But there are certain strands that are quite constant — two, very briefly. The good life for Confucianism involves the pursuit of compassionate social relations. And that's really key. It's not an otherworldly philosophy. There's hardly anything about the afterlife. And it's really about how we should learn to engage and to love and also be responsible in our social relations. There's also an issue about the best life, (which) involves serving the community, so people love to, well, compete to be public officials in order to have that opportunity to serve the community.

Another value which has been revived is the value in Chinese "礼." In English, we can translate it as "ritual propriety." The idea is that we can use laws to regulate people to stop them from doing bad things. But if we really want to have a kind of harmonious society, that comes to informal mechanisms, like rituals that generate a sense of community. So, this is one reason why the idea of ritual propriety has been revived in different spheres of social and even political life in China.

Another value that's been revived a lot is filial piety, "孝," which we can also translate as reverence for elderly members of the family and ancestors. So one of the festivals that has been revived in China is called the Qingming Festival, the ancestor worship festival. And this is sort of thing that evolved from the bottom. Literally, hundreds of millions of ordinary Chinese people took the day off on that particular day to worship their ancestors. And eventually, the government said, "Well, fine, let's just make it into a national holiday." So, a lot of this revival comes from the bottom up, not just from the top.

That said, some of the reasons for the revival are political, because (of) the top leaders and also the middle-level leaders like, for us, the bureaucracy in Shandong Province. In order to seek, to think about, to make sense of our social and political system, we draw on the earlier Confucian tradition and some of the values that inspires [inspired] us in the past. And also it continues to inspire us in the future. So that's one reason for the revival of Confucianism. It comes from the top.

But there are also many economic reasons. I mean why has East Asia evolved in a relatively peaceful and harmonious way relative to other countries? Well, it turns out that most of those countries have a Confucian heritage, not just China, but South Korea and Singapore. So what is it? People used to blame that the 20th century ... people blamed the backwardness of China for ... they said, (it's) because of our traditions, but then it turns out that actually those traditions help us to modernize in a relatively peaceful way. Values like self-improvement, working for future generations, education of this worldly outlook ... all these values underpin China's economic growth and form of modernization, which has taken place in the past 30 or 40 years, without a great deal of, well, violence and social disruption compared to many other countries.

But also, frankly, economic growth tends to make people more individualistic, especially in a capitalist-influenced economy. So there are certainly people who worry about excessive individualism in society. How do we counter that? Well, Confucianism is beautiful in this way, because it emphasizes our social responsibilities. So as a wave of, let's say, countering excessive individualism in society, Confucianism has also made a comeback for that reason.

There is [are] also academic reasons. I mean ... It turns out that many of the defenders of Confucianism today were forced to read it 30 or 40 years ago in order to denounce it, because it was viewed as a kind of feudal and backward thought system. But when they read it, they says [said] this is actually far more interesting and complex and actually modern-sounding than we thought. And then once (the country) was more opening, those same intellectuals could draw on Confucianism and say that this is not only relevant for the modern world, but we can also use it to inspire our social and political reform in the future.

So this is why, again, Confucianism (is) far from being a backward, conservative philosophy. It's actually quite modern and desirable for the modern world. Confucianism, as a living tradition, is inspiring, not just for the present, but for the future as well. It's as valuable as other great traditions that humans have produced, including Christianity, Islam, Buddhism, liberalism. And if you take it seriously, it turns out that it's a tradition, not just that has produced great thinkers in the past, but that, I believe, will continue to inspire us in the future as well.

五、补充阅读

1）Moser-Mercer, B. (2008). Skill acquisition in interpreting: A human performance perspective. *The Interpreter and Translator Trainer*, 2(1), 1-28.

2）雷天放，陈菁. 口译教程 [M]. 上海：上海外语教育出版社，2006.

测试和总结

一、测试说明

1）测试形式：
- 口头回答关于某口译技能的问题（四选一），即兴演讲2~3分钟。
- 源语复述一个2分钟的讲话。

2）要求：有理有据，逻辑清晰，表达得当。

3）测试后填写"评估与反思"部分的自评表和总结。

4）成绩构成：问答占30%，复述占50%，按时提交自评表和总结占20%。

二、测试题

1）问答题

You will be given four questions. Choose one to answer right on the spot. You have one minute to prepare before the recording starts. Be sure to talk to the point and be logical and clear.

2）复述题

You are going to listen to a two-minute interview about working from home. It is divided into three segments. Please retell the message in English after you hear the stop signal.

生词表

英文	中文
hustle and bustle	拥挤不堪
camaraderie	友情，同事情谊
sortie	（短暂）外出，出门
inverted commas	引号

三、评估与反思

无笔记训练自测评估表

姓名： 总分：

第一题（30分，知识掌握和限时表达能力: 100% = 知识60% + 表达40%）

请将录音转成文字（含题目）	
Length: _____ Word count: _____ Rate: _____ per minute Number of unnecessary fillers (er, oh, etc.): _____	
Grades	Please briefly assess and grade your performance considering the following aspects.
Self-grading: _____	Did you speak in a correct and comprehensive manner? (0–18分)
Self-grading: _____	Did you answer the question logically and clearly? (0–12分)
Total score:（前两项之和） _____	Did you give a good speech? Why or why not? A brief comment on your performance:

第二题（50分，结构理解/信息点理解和记忆检查: 100% = 信息70% +表达30%）

请将录音转成文字		
复述:		
Grades	**Please fill in the form with brief comments.**	
Information（30分） Self-grading: _____	Main idea（20分）	Sub-points of information（10分）
Delivery（20分） Self-grading: _____	Voice Quality: Pleasant / Normal / Not Pleasing Voice Clarity: Clear / Normal / Unclear Fillers: Few / Some / Many Pauses: Few / Some / Many	
Total score:（前两 项之和） _____	Please briefly comment on your performance (logic, delivery, etc.) Are there any wrong messages in your interpreting?	

第三题（10分）

自我小结		
做得好的地方	做得不够好的地方	改进方法

第四题（10分）

无笔记训练阶段学习总结和反思

笔记训练

第6章 ▶ 笔记基本问题

一、技能解说

1）交传笔记本身具有个性化、暂存性质。笔记是记忆的载体，但不是信息的文字化。笔记的作用在于，在记录时帮助译员集中精力、在使用笔记时起提示作用。（塞莱斯科维奇、勒代雷，1989）。

2）为什么要记笔记？

✔ 减少脑记负担（to relieve memory）；

✔ 激活脑记（to jog memory）。

3）笔记的地位：

✔ 笔记是次要的；

✔ 笔记仅是手段，不是目的；

✔ 笔记本质上是个人化的。

4）笔记应当记什么内容？

✔ 大意及大意之间的联系；

✔ 脑记容易忘记的，如讲话开头和结尾；

✔ 脑记记不住的，如专有名词、数字、人名、地名等。

二、训练方法

● 做无笔记复述训练之后，尝试把脑记的内容浓缩成几个字、词或符号写到纸上，边看边回忆刚才脑记的内容，再复述。反思这几个浓缩的字、词或符号是否有助于提示脑记内容。总结有效的字、词或符号。

● 听自己的无笔记复述录音。将遗漏的信息或细节用笔记下来，反思信息遗漏的原因。分析原因，找解决办法。比如：

✔ 没听懂（需要进一步练习听大意的能力）

✔ 脑记没记住数字、专有名词、人名、地名等细节信息（思考笔记中如何有效记下这些信息）

✔ 复述的时候忘了（思考如何用笔记激活记忆）

● 尝试在符号和笔记的帮助下进行口译练习。在小组中分享自己是怎么记笔记的、效果如何等。

● 在笔记的辅助下，继续进行单纯数字练习，如含million或billion的数字。

三、练习案例点评

───────────────────── 案例1 ─────────────────────

源　　语：With pleasure. I think there are at least two differences in the way of business communication between Chinese and American businessmen. First, Chinese businessmen tend to have business negotiations in a rather indirect manner, as opposed to the more direct manner of American businessmen. The Chinese take time to learn if their prospective business contacts are really reliable, for example, by inviting them to a party and socializing with them. In contrast, the Americans act with the "get-down-to-business-first" mentality. Second, the decision-making process of Chinese companies is generally slow and time-consuming. This is because most Chinese companies keep to the "bottom-up, then top-down, and then bottom-up" decision-making principle which involves many people at different levels. American companies, on the other hand, usually operate with quick decisions made by the top management. I hope American businessmen in China will understand these differences in business practices and adjust to the Chinese way.

学生译语：好的，我认为，嗯，中国生意人和美国生意人在商务交流方式上有两点不同。第一，中国生意人比较含蓄，而美国生意人则比较直接。中国生意人会通过，嗯，开派对来谈生意。相反，美国生意人则采取直接沟通的方式。第二，中国公司的决策过程慢，这是因为中国公司采取的是……上情下达、再由领导层做决定、再把决定传达给下属的这样一个过程，而美国公司做决定则是由领导层直接做决定。我希望美国生意人能够理解商务交流方式上的不同并且调整、适应它。

📖 点评

1）大意译出来了，但丢失了一些细节，有些表达不准确，还有"嗯"和一处超过三秒的停顿。

2）原文中提到The Chinese take time to learn if their prospective business contacts are really reliable, for example by inviting them to a party and socializing with them，而译语中仅仅提及中国生意人会通过开派对来谈生意，并不准确。

3）细节上有漏译，which involves many people at different levels、usually operate with quick decisions中的quick、American businessmen in China中的in China没译出来。

教师评分：85。

源　语：Harvard University President Lawrence Summers announced last week that he will resign as of June 30. The former Treasury Secretary has led the nation's oldest and richest university for five years.

Education experts say one of his main difficulties was a power struggle with professors who control undergraduate education.

The Faculty of Arts and Sciences had been expected to consider a measure this week expressing a lack of support in his leadership.

学生译语：上周，哈佛大学校长宣布将在6月30号辞职，他选择离开这所世界上最古老的、享受声誉以及资金充足的学校。此前，他担任这一职位长达5年。一些教育专家指出他主要的困难是权力斗争，这种斗争主要是和教授本科生的教授之间的，他们掌握着本科生毕业的权力。这周，该校长表达了自己在领导层面缺乏支持。

📋 点评

1）译语大意完整，三层大意都译出来了。但细节信息有遗漏，如the former Treasury Secretary。

2）最后一句话的意思理解错误，主语应为the Faculty of Arts and Sciences，也没有正确理解expressing a lack of support in his leadership的含义。

3）人称指代不够清楚：比如校长的名字一直用"他"重复；"他们掌握着本科生毕业的权力"中的"他们"指代不明。

4）整体来看，译语句子较为零散，源语一句话在译语中有时被拆分成了好几句。这样的句子信息密度较小，包含的有效信息不多，可能让听众不耐烦。应该进行信息整合，使汉语表达简洁凝练。

教师评分：75。

四、篇章练习

生词表

英文	中文
sexist	性别歧视者
rehabilitation program	（戒除毒品、酒精等成瘾物质的）康复项目

1）Business communication styles

练习说明：

1. This is an interview with an American manager of a Sino-American joint venture on some of the differences in business communication styles and work ethics between the Chinese and the Americans.

2. The interview is divided into five segments. Please take notes and interpret only the English parts into Chinese. Record your interpretation at each stop signal. Here's a tip for you: Remember that in interviews, the message of a question matches that of its answer.

3. After interpreting, review your recording for quality: Does your interpretation contain any language fillers, pauses longer than three seconds, disorganized information, or unidiomatic expressions?

4. Interpret it again without notes, and compare your interpretations. Consider the following questions: Did your notes help with your memory? If so, how did they help? If not, why were they ineffective? What did you take down, and did you keep them to the minimum necessary? Compare your notes with those of your peers and discuss how to take notes better.

Q: 您好，杰克逊先生。您在中国已连续工作了三年，您能否谈一下中美两国生意人在商务沟通方式上有何不同之处？

A: With pleasure. I think there are at least two differences in the way of business communication between Chinese and American businessmen. First, Chinese businessmen tend to have business negotiations in a rather indirect manner, as opposed to the more direct manner of American businessmen. The Chinese take time to learn if their prospective business contacts are really reliable, for example, by inviting them to a party and socializing with them. In contrast, the Americans act with the "get-down-to-business-first" mentality. Second, the decision-making process of Chinese companies is generally slow and time-consuming. This is because most Chinese companies keep to the "bottom-up, then top-down, and then bottom-up" decision-making principle which involves many people at different levels. American companies, on the other hand, usually operate with quick decisions made by the top management. I hope American businessmen in China will understand these differences in business practices and adjust to the Chinese way.

Q: 美国式的经营之道在我们中国人看来常显得咄咄逼人。您在与中国同事合作中有无注意到这一点？

A: Well, we are more direct and straightforward than most Chinese, I would say, due to our different cultural traditions. I noticed that a lot of Chinese often avoid saying a clear "no" just to be polite. Sometimes my Chinese colleagues say "yes" not to express agreement, but only to show that they are listening.

Q: 我们都应该承认这些文化差异，尊重这些差异，以免产生误解。这很重要，不是吗？

A: Yes, understanding these differences, I believe, will be a first step toward establishing a firm business relationship between American and Chinese companies.

Q: 刚才您提到了中国式的决策过程，您认为这种管理模式有无优点？将其与美国式的管理模式相比，您有何看法？

A: I would say the American-type, or the top-down management, emphasizes efficiency and competition among workers, while the Chinese-type management gives priority to careful planning and encourages cooperation among workers, and between workers and the management. Thus, while the American-type management often frustrates many workers, the Chinese-type management gives workers a joy of participation and fulfillment, and a sense of pride in their work.

Q: 谈到员工的工作态度，中国人和美国人在这方面有何不同？

A: I think most Chinese view work as essential for having membership in a community. They believe that work allows them to have the sense of belonging to a community. In other words, work is necessary for them to gain social acceptance in the society. That is why many Chinese managers and employees work so hard to maintain their positions in their companies. Also, they see work as the most important thing in life. That is, they have tried to find the meaning of life through their jobs. While the Chinese work ethic is based on social pressure and community belonging, the American work ethic seems to be more individual-oriented. We often value the results and accomplishments of work more than its process. By the way, I'm very impressed by the obvious strong sense of dedication to the jobs among the Chinese employees.

Q: 回到我们一开始的话题，您如何评价中美两种不同经营之道的利弊？

A: It is difficult to decide which is better than which, because there are some merits and demerits to [of] both types of management. My suggestion is that people of both countries should learn from each other. I will say that in recent years, the merits of the Chinese way, or rather, the Oriental way, of management are beginning to be recognized by an increasing number of people in the West. This more humane Oriental way of management seems to offer a great deal to the executives of our American industries.

2）Harvard president was going to resign

练习说明：

1. This is an educational news report titled "Summers Resigns After Five Years as Harvard President." Brainstorm the causes of his resignation. What do you expect to be challenging when interpreting this report? Please prepare beforehand.

2. The report is divided into four segments. Interpret the message at each stop signal and record your interpretation.

3. After interpreting,
   1) review your recording for quality: Does your interpretation contain any language fillers, pauses longer than three seconds, disorganized information, or unidiomatic expressions?
   2) share your notes with your peers to discuss ways to improve note-taking for better interpretation.

Harvard University President Lawrence Summers announced last week that he will resign as of June 30. The former Treasury Secretary has led the nation's oldest and richest university for five years.

Education experts say one of his main difficulties was a power struggle with professors who control undergraduate education.

The Faculty of Arts and Sciences had been expected to consider a measure this week expressing a lack of support in his leadership. He lost a similar no-confidence vote a year ago. That happened after he suggested that biological differences may be a reason for the few women in top science and math jobs. Critics called him "sexist."

Mr. Summers apologized. But his comments led Harvard to begin working toward increasing the number of women in science.

Soon after he arrived at Harvard, he angered minority groups by criticizing Cornel West, a well-known black studies professor. Mr. Summers accused him of grading his students too highly and not carrying out serious research. The dispute led Mr. West to leave Harvard for Princeton University.

Mr. Summers also criticized grade inflation in other classes. A recent conflict involved the resignation of Arts and Sciences Dean William Kirby. Some professors believe Mr. Summers dismissed him. Mr. Kirby has said it was a joint decision.

Opponents say Mr. Summers was not able to lead the university effectively. Supporters say he made too many enemies as he worked to improve the university by changing it.

Among his efforts, Mr. Summers helped make it possible for more students from poor families to attend Harvard. Yet some experts on higher education say his experience at Harvard could affect reform efforts at other schools.

The Harvard student newspaper, *The (Harvard) Crimson*, recently asked undergraduates how they felt about Mr. Summers' leadership. Fifty-seven percent said they supported him. Nineteen percent wanted him to leave.

The university is now searching for a new leader. Former President Derek Bok will serve until one is found.

Mr. Summers plans to spend a year away from Harvard and return as an economics professor. Harvard is in Cambridge, Massachusetts. It was established in 1636. Gifts and investments have increased its endowment wealth to more than 25,000 million dollars.

3 ）Distraction

练习说明：

1. This is a talk about the psychology of distraction and a few techniques to stay on track. Brainstorm before listening: What will be covered in this talk? How could these ideas be possibly linked logically?
2. The talk is divided into seven segments. Take notes and interpret at each stop signal, and record your interpretation.
3. After interpreting,
   1) review your recording for quality: Does your interpretation contain any language fillers, pauses longer than three seconds, disorganized information, or unidiomatic expressions?
   2) reflect on your notes when listening to your interpretation. What did you take down? Did your notes help improve your memory and how?
   3) think about the following questions: Did you find any words difficult to understand, let alone to interpret? How did you manage to cope with them by context and find appropriate Chinese equivalence? Discuss your solution with your peers.

My name is Nir Eyal, and I've spent the last five years researching and writing about the deeper psychology of distraction. When I found myself struggling with distraction, I decided to do what many people advise and got rid of the distracting technology. I got myself a flip phone without any apps. All it did was phone calls and text messages. Then I got a word processor from the 1990s without any sort of Internet connection. Unfortunately, I found I still got distracted.

I'd start reading a book from my bookshelf. I'd tidy up my desk. I'd take out the trash even — just to avoid the thing that I didn't want to do.

I had only focused on the external triggers — the pings and dings that were leading me towards distraction. What I hadn't focused on, and what turns out to be a much more common source of distraction, are the internal triggers — the uncomfortable emotional states that we seek to escape. When we're lonely, we check Facebook. When we're uncertain, we google. When we're bored, we check the news, stocks prices, sports scores — anything to not feel these uncomfortable sensations that we're not ready to experience.

Here are a few techniques I discovered in my research that could help us stay on track.

[1. Plan your day (but not with a to-do list)]
First what you want to do is to make sure you plan your day. Two-thirds of people don't keep any sort of calendar, (or) any kind of schedule in their day. Well, the fact of the matter is if you don't plan your day, somebody is going to plan it for you.

Many of us believe in this myth of the to-do list. I used to think that just by writing things down they'd get done. But of course, I'd go from day to day to day recycling the bottom half of my to-do list because I wasn't making time to do those tasks. So the best place to start is not with the output of what you want to get done every day but with the input of how much time you have to devote to every task.

[2. Use social media and email at set times]
So distraction has many consequences. One of them is that we find that when someone is interrupted during a task, it can take up to 20 minutes for them to refocus on what they were doing. Many times we don't even realize how much worse our output is when we … So check email in one solid block. If you enjoy using social media, that's great, but make time for it in your day so it's not something you're only using every time you feel bored or lonely.

[3. Surf the urge]
Researchers have found that surfing the urge is an effective way to master our internal triggers. In a smoking cessation study, researchers found that when they taught smokers how to notice the

sensation and be mindful of what they were experiencing, they became much more likely to stop smoking. By surfing the urge and noticing what it is that we're experiencing and allowing that sensation to crest and then subside — kind of like how a surfer might surf a wave — we allow that emotion, that uncomfortable internal trigger, to crest and then pass.

[4. Beware of "liminal moments"]

The next thing that we want to do is (to) be careful of "liminal moments." Liminal moments are these periods of time when we are transitioning from one task to the other. So for example, if you start checking your email on the way back from a meeting, and you're finally at your desk, and you keep checking your email instead of getting to the task at hand, well, now that liminal moment has turned into a distraction. So be careful of those times when you're transitioning from one task to the next.

[5. Remember you're not powerless]

A study of alcoholics found that the number one determinant of whether someone would stay sober after a rehabilitation program was not their level of physical dependency. It wasn't what was happening in their ~~body~~ [bodies]. In fact, it was what was happening in their minds. The people who were most likely to stay sober were those who believed they had the power to stop.

So when we think that technology is hijacking our brains, or it's addicting everyone, we are making it more likely that we won't be able to put technology distractions in their place. So don't believe this lie that there's nothing we can do. Clearly, there's so much we can do to help make sure that we get the best out of these products without letting them get the best of us.

五、补充阅读

1）Gillies, A. (2009). *Note-taking for Consecutive Interpreting: A Short Course*. Shanghai: Shanghai Foreign Language Education Press.

2）刘敏华. 逐步口译与笔记：理论、实践与教学 [M]. 台北：书林出版有限公司，2008.

3）仲伟合，王斌华. 基础口译 [M]. 北京：外语教学与研究出版社，2009.

第7章 ▶ 记大意

一、技能解说

1）笔记格式：

✓ SVO结构，对角线方向记录关键信息（diagonal layout noting down main ideas based on a subject-verb-object analysis）；

✓ 左侧留白（left-hand margin）；

✓ 竖状排列列举内容（verticality of lists）；

✓ 适当用缩略语和符号（abbreviations and symbols）。

2）笔记语言：倾向于用目的语（target language）记；在不影响听和理解的条件下，哪种语言来得快就用哪种语言记。

3）笔记时刻：听懂意思再动手记；预测到即将有数字或列举内容时，集中精力迅速记下数字或列举内容。

4）读笔记：看一眼笔记，抬头看着听众口译，再看一眼笔记，再抬头讲。不能一直看着笔记说话。

二、训练方法

● 将无笔记训练中脑记的内容概括为标签（tagging）。把这个标签记到笔记中，口译时眼睛看着这个标签，看它能否提示一长串脑记的信息。如果能，这个标签就是合适的笔记。

● 明确听懂、分析、脑记之后再笔记。笔记一开始越少越好，一个字或词代表一串信息。根据笔记的提示，回忆起脑记的内容，再复述或翻译。小组练习笔记口译，互相交流，反复体会理解、脑记和笔记的关系，找感觉、找问题，并记录问题，便于交流和提问。

● 练习笔记带各种度量衡单位的数字，如将five hundred U.S. dollars记为$500等。

三、练习案例点评

—————————————— 案例1 ——————————————

源　　语：This year, April 17 is the last day for Americans to pay federal income taxes for

2005. Most taxpayers have enough income tax collected by their employers during the year, so they do not owe any more money. In fact, most Americans get some money back. Last year, the Internal Revenue Service returned at least some money to more than 100 million Americans paying individual income tax.

The United States has what is called a progressive tax system. Tax rates increase as earnings increase. This year, people earning more than 326,000 dollars are taxed at the highest rate. Earnings above that amount are taxed at 35 percent; earnings below that amount are taxed at lower rates. Individuals who earn less than 7,300 dollars pay no income tax, but they do pay Social Security, Medicare, and other taxes.

学生译语： 17号是美国人在今年缴纳2005年联邦所得税的最后一天。大多数美国人已经通过雇主缴纳了足够多的税款，并不再欠任何税款。事实上，许多美国人收到了返款。去年，国税局为至少一亿美国人退还了部分个人所得税。美国采用递进式税收制度，收入越高，税率越高。今年，收入达三十二万六千美元的人将缴纳最高税率的税款。年收入大于三十二万六千美元的人需要以百分之三十五的税率缴税，低于这一数字的人则缴纳较低的税。收入低于七千三百美元的人无须缴纳个人所得税，但仍须缴纳社保、医疗税。

📋 点评

1）译语中"年收入大于三十二万六千美元的人需要以百分之三十五的税率缴税"信息理解有误，应当是"年收入超过三十二万六千美元的部分按百分之三十五的税率纳税"。

2）April漏译。年代、日期等时间表述，如This year、April 17，放到最前面说更符合中文习惯，成句也能更流畅。

3）部分用词不够正式。比如，说"最后期限"相比"最后一天"更正式。"返款"不如"税收返还"正式。应当看着笔记边想边说，监控输出语表达，不要完全受限于原文用词的字面对应。

4）"美国国税局"不能说成"国税局"，因为听众是中国人。

教师评分：87。

--- **案例2** ---

源　语： There are many different ways for people and businesses to reduce their federal income taxes. Most homeowners, for example, can reduce their taxes a little by reporting to the IRS the interest they pay on a home loan. This is called a tax deduction.

Companies deduct many costs involved in doing business. And many industries can deduct costs of research, exploring for natural resources, and the use of property and equipment.

学生译语： 对个人和企业来说，有很多方式可以减少税收。对持家者来说，他们可以通过上报IRS来减少自己要交的税。这就是降税。公司的很多业务也可以得到降税。对工厂来说，它们做研究，开发资源以及使用装备也可以实现降税。

📋 点评

1）总体不错，大意译出来了；表达有点啰嗦，停顿太多。

2）"对……来说"这样的表达显得句子重复，这个结构本身意义不大，直接说"个人和企业可以采取很多方式实现减税"更加简洁。

3）有些用词不够准确。比如，homeowner不应译为"持家者"，应译为"买房者"；比起"开发资源"，译为"资源勘探"会稍好些；tax reduction不应译为"降税"，应译为"减税"。

4）home loan这个信息点漏译。

教师评分：88。

四、篇章练习

生词表

英文	中文
Internal Revenue Service, IRS	美国国家税务局
tax deduction	税收减免
Diagnostic and Statistical Manual of Mental Disorders, DSM	《精神疾病诊断与统计手册》
compulsivity	强制性
cold turkey	快速戒断（突然彻底戒断上瘾物的治疗方法）
detox	脱瘾
carpentry	木工活，木工工艺
flunk out	（因不及格而）被退学
breastfeeding	母乳喂养
American Academy of Pediatrics	美国儿科学会
gynecologist	妇科医生
carbohydrate	碳水化合物
fatty acid	脂肪酸
whey	乳清

（待续）

（续表）

英文	中文
casein	酪蛋白
electrolyte	电解质
pancreas	胰腺
diarrhea	腹泻
respiratory infection	呼吸道感染
urinary tract infection	尿道感染
gastral and intestinal tract	胃肠道
colitis	结肠炎
ulcerative	溃疡性的
allergy	过敏
asthma	哮喘
allergen	过敏原
ovulation	排卵
ovarian cancer	卵巢癌
La Leche League	国际母乳协会
colostrum	初乳

1）Tax time in the U.S.

练习说明：

1. This is a news report on the tax system in the U.S. Brainstorm before listening: What do you know about the tax policies in the U.S. and in China? What kind of information do you expect to be included in this report? How do you anticipate the main ideas or sub-ideas to be connected in this report? Consider numbers, measurement units, and proper names that may appear in this report.

2. The report is divided into five segments. Interpret the message at each stop signal and record your interpretation.

3. After interpreting,

   1) review your recording for quality: Does your interpretation contain any language fillers, pauses longer than three seconds, disorganized information, or unidiomatic expressions? When you were interpreting, were you able to maintain eye contact with the audience while only referring to your notes occasionally?

   2) reflect on your notes and think about the following questions:

- Did you take notes in a proper form? How did you note down the links between ideas? Discuss your notes with your peers and think about how to improve them.
- How well did you interpret the numbers? What difficulties have you met in number interpreting? Do you find the numbers, their measurements, and the context in conflict with each other in your interpretation? Discuss with your peers how to solve these problems.

This year, April 17 is the last day for Americans to pay federal income taxes for 2005. Most taxpayers have had enough income tax collected by their employers during the year, so they do not owe any more money. In fact, most Americans get some money back. Last year, the Internal Revenue Service returned at least some money to more than 100 million Americans paying individual income tax.

The United States has what is called a progressive tax system. Tax rates increase as earnings increase. This year, people earning more than 326,000 dollars are taxed at the highest rate. Earnings above that amount are taxed at 35 percent; earnings below that amount are taxed at lower rates. Individuals who earn less than 7,300 dollars pay no income tax, but they do pay Social Security, Medicare, and other taxes.

There are many different ways for people and businesses to reduce their federal income taxes. Most homeowners, for example, can reduce their taxes a little by reporting to the IRS the interest they pay on a home loan. This is called a tax deduction.

Companies deduct many costs involved in doing business. And many industries can deduct costs of research, exploring for natural resources, and the use of property and equipment.

In 2004, personal income taxes provided the government with most of its money: 35 percent of the budget. Social Security and other retirement taxes provided 32 percent. Other forms of income include business income taxes, money borrowed to cover the deficit, and special taxes on trade and property.

But income from taxes did not provide enough to pay for government spending. The IRS says the budget deficit for 2004 was about 400,000 million dollars.

Preparing tax documents can be complex. The IRS estimates that taxpayers need an average of about 13 hours to prepare tax documents. And that is just for the basic tax form. For businesses, the IRS estimates an average tax preparer needs more than 50 hours. This is why a lot of

Americans pay professional tax preparers to complete their tax documents for them.

2）Without a net

练习说明：

1. This is a radio program talking about the first Internet addiction treatment center in the U.S. In the program, the host speaks to the executive director of the center and her recent patient Ben Alexander. Brainstorm before listening: What are they possibly going to talk about? And how will the conversation be carried out? Do you know any terms about video games and Internet addiction?

2. Their conversation is divided into nine segments. Record your interpretation at each stop signal.

3. After interpreting,

   1) review your recording for quality: Does your interpretation contain any language fillers, pauses longer than three seconds, disorganized information, or unidiomatic expressions?

   2) check your notes against your interpretation. Did you take notes in a proper form? Did you note down the links on the left-hand margin? Did you find the interview style in which the host puts forward an opinion, and the interviewee supports, proves or illustrates it, helps you better understand and memorize the ideas? Discuss your notes with your peers and think about how to improve them.

Host: In November of 2008, the Chinese Health Ministry recognized Internet addiction as a medical diagnosis. That country, one of the first to establish treatment centers for the disorder, now has hundreds of clinics set up to help people get offline.

Here in the States, we're more skeptical of the diagnosis, but now we do have one treatment program, reSTART, which calls itself "an Internet addiction recovery program." Hilarie Cash is the executive director of reSTART. Welcome to the show.

Hilarie Cash: Glad to be here, thank you.

Host: So define "Internet addiction." Is it a clinical term?

Hilarie Cash: It's not an official clinical term, yet. We do know that in the next version of the *DSM* they are going to have a category for non-substance-use addictions, and we know that gambling is going to be there. What other behavioral addictions make their way into that is entirely dependent on the weight of evidence. But all behavioral addictions have certain things in common with substance addictions — loss of control, or compulsivity about engaging in ~~it~~ [them], the development of tolerance, the experience of withdrawal, and the engagement in ~~it~~ [them] in spite of negative consequences.

Host: Now, you already have your first patient, who right now is undergoing treatment at the facility. Can you tell me about Ben Alexander?

Hilarie Cash: Ben, I think in many ways, is going to be a typical client. He's 19. He has social anxiety. He found that going online to socialize was where he preferred to be rather than sort of out in the world and dating and hanging out with friends. It didn't matter too much while he was still under the structure of his family, but once he went off to college, he really just fell right down that rabbit hole into an addictive pattern where he barely went to classes and, slowly over time, began to fail out.

Host: Can you tell me what Ben's treatment has been like? I mean, I understand that when you're dealing with alcoholics or people who suffer from a gambling addiction, the tendency would be to go cold turkey. Can you prescribe cold turkey to your clients?

Hilarie Cash: We do prescribe cold turkey. This really is an opportunity for them to spend 45 days free of the Internet. It gives their brains a chance to kind of detox and begin to rewire into more normal patterns. So he'll get up in the morning, have breakfast. He'll be involved then in house chores, cleaning up, gardening, care of animals, that kind of thing. After that, there's physical exercise. Many of the activities in the afternoon are centered around vocational therapy. They're working right now on developing his carpentry skills. And then in the evening, there ~~is~~ [are] mindfulness training, 12-step work, and other addiction-related work.

Host: Now, I know Ben is your first client, but if he is, as you say, typical of who you expect to come into your program, aren't his problems really separate from the Internet? I mean, if you were to, say, treat him for his social anxiety disorder and whatever other problems that he takes with him to the Internet, then he wouldn't need to be cured of an Internet addiction. Isn't that much more of a symptom than it is a cause?

Hilarie Cash: What people often don't understand is that addiction becomes its own problem. You do indeed need to address those root problems, but actually it becomes very difficult to address them effectively as long as the addiction is active.

Host: Ben Alexander has just completed the forty-five-day treatment and he joins me now. Ben, welcome to the show.

Ben Alexander: Thank you.

Host: Tell me about your drug of choice.

Ben Alexander: Well, it's a massively multiplayer online role-playing game, which basically means that you play with people from all around the world, and you have this kind of character that you create that represents you in the world.

Host: What about it did you find so addictive?

Ben Alexander: Well, part of it was the social aspect. It's a very social game, and a lot of working together with other people to complete objectives and things like that. And I've always dealt with a lot of social anxiety… And it was just a lot easier to… to be comfortable socializing online than it ever was in real life for me.

Host: You didn't feel, like, the kind of ease that you had in the game could translate to the real world?

Ben Alexander: Not at the time, no. I've been doing a lot more getting out and meeting people in real life, and it's been easier than I thought it would be.

Host: Can you describe what the moment was, if there was a moment, when you realized that you really had a problem?

Ben Alexander: Yeah, it was about halfway through my first semester in college, and I realized that if I kept doing what I was doing, which was pretty much ~~play~~ [playing] a game all day, every day, I was going to flunk out of college.

Host: But you couldn't stop?

Ben Alexander: No, I couldn't. My dad tried to help. I went to him and asked for his help and he tried to help me set up rules about when I could play, and … I mean, none of it worked.

Host: How many days since you left the center?

Ben Alexander: Three days.

Host: Three days. And are you nervous? Are you pretty comfortable? Are you confident?

Ben Alexander: I am. Right now my parents have it set up where I have access to their computer and I can get online for work-related things and also for reconnecting with friends that I've kind of lost contact with.

Host: So, Ben, good luck.
Ben Alexander: Thank you.

3）Is breastfeeding best for newborns?

练习说明：

1. This is a broadcast in which the hostess discusses with Dr. Judith Reichman the benefits of breastfeeding. Brainstorm before listening: What do you know about breastfeeding and other ways to feed newborns? What are the pros and cons of breastfeeding in your opinion? What might be covered in the broadcast and what might be the logic framework of their discussion?

2. The broadcast is divided into 11 segments. Interpret the message at each stop signal and record your interpretation.

3. After interpreting,

   1) review your recording for quality: Does your interpretation contain any language fillers, pauses longer than three seconds, disorganized information, or unidiomatic expressions?

   2) check your notes against your interpretation. Did you take notes in the form of SVO? How did you take down the main ideas and sub-ideas? Did your notes on numbers and names work well to help produce better Chinese interpretation? Discuss your notes with your peers.

Hostess: This morning on Today's Woman, the benefits of breastfeeding. Nursing is a wonderful way to bond with the newborn and get them off to a healthy start as well, but according to a recent report from the American Academy of Pediatrics, less than 60 percent of women breastfed their newborn at the time they were discharged from the hospital. Dr. Judith Reichman is a gynecologist and contributor here of today. Hey, Judith. Good morning.

Dr. Reichman: Good morning.

Hostess: So I'm just looking at less than 60 percent …

Dr. Reichman: And that's when they left the hospital and less than 21 percent were breastfeeding at (the) sixth month and many of them were supplementing … They weren't doing sole breastfeeding.

Hostess: So why do you think these numbers are so low?

Dr. Reichman: I think it's very difficult for the working women to breastfeed and sometimes there is difficulty in initiating it. I'm not sure that everybody realizes how truly important to the health, both of the baby and the mother, it is.

Hostess: Why and what about formula? Is it as beneficial to the baby? Could modern-day formula (be the same) as mom's milk?

Dr. Reichman: Well. I'm gonna use this phrase that I often use — "breast is best" — and it really is. The milk that comes from the breast has the absolute right amount of carbohydrates, proteins, vitamins, fatty acids, minerals … You can't do better and we don't even know everything that's in breast milk so formula can't really, totally copy it. But it certainly is much better than cow's milk which has things in it that the baby simply cannot and should not digest.

Hostess: Well. You can't give a newborn cow's milk, right?

Dr. Reichman: You absolutely should not. The protein in the cow's milk is wrong. Breast milk has something called whey and casein, and the whey is way above the amount (of the casein). It's about 72 percent. Cow's milk is just the opposite. It has the wrong currents of electrolyte. It has a protein in it which actually can cause changes in the beta cells of the pancreas and help increase risk of diabetes in an infant or in a child.

Hostess: OK. So breast milk, though, is on a positive side. Breast milk can prevent diarrhea, respiratory infections, ear infections, and urinary tract infections.

Dr. Reichman: It has wonderful antibodies and has cells that eat up the bad bacteria. It coats the lining of the gastral and intestinal tract. It prevents bad proteins from getting in, and it actually decreases colitis and ulcerative colitis down the line.

Hostess: Also … and we talked about allergies here. We hear more about allergies these days, many more kids being diagnosed with asthma. And there is some evidence that breastfeeding can help stave off this condition?

Dr. Reichman: Yes. It's thought that if a woman exclusively breastfeeds for six months, she can decrease the allergens. She gives antibodies. If she doesn't eat nuts for example, then the baby is less likely to get the allergies to nuts. So the American Academy of Pediatrics suggests that all women who have a history of allergies or asthma in their family breastfeed exclusively for six months.

Hostess:	Also mental development. There ~~has~~ [have] been studies that show that breastfed babies are smarter, right?
Dr. Reichman:	Yeah. Well. I wasn't breastfed, so I keep thinking had I been breastfed who knows what I would have done.
Hostess:	You've been brilliant. You already are … You would be too scary.
Dr. Reichman:	But in many cases there is some thought that it increases cognition and that these children not only are a little smarter but the smartness continues down the line. So the longer a child is breastfed, maybe the better the brain develops.
Hostess:	Yeah. Come to think that I wasn't breastfed either. See? Think where we'll be today and (what) will happen. All right, what about childhood obesity?
Dr. Reichman:	There are definitely some suggestions that it decreases obesity and also it decreases diabetes as I said before.

Hostess:	What about ~~for~~ the mom? I know that it delays the onset of your first period, but it also can help you burn a lot of calories after your pregnancy, right?
Dr. Reichman:	It's much easier to lose that baby weight if you breastfeed, and that's probably one of the chief reasons women are anxious to do it. But in addition, it decreases the amount of bleeding after delivery. It decreases ovulation. She's less likely to get breast cancer and ovarian cancer.

Hostess:	Well, the one thing I want to mention, though, too, is it's difficult to breastfeed. And I don't think new mothers are told this. It doesn't sort of necessarily, instantaneously happen where the baby latches on. So people should know that there're experts in hospitals. There's the La Leche League. I know. I've got a pump from them.
Dr. Reichman:	But you know what, the more you do it — you really do it — the better you get out of it. And we really tell mothers ~~trying do~~ [to try doing] it every two hours. If you don't get enough milk out, try again. Use a pump. Learn what you can do.

Hostess:	But talk to the experts because as I said I think a lot of women find it very frustrating and there are people on the hospital staff that you should talk to even before you have your baby. If you're interested in breastfeeding, just say, "Will you be available if I have any problems?"

Dr. Reichman: Absolutely, and the first breastfeeding is probably the most important because at that time the colostrum comes out. And that's chock-full of antibodies and good things for the baby, so the hospital has to make sure that the baby room is available and they have to help the mother nurse, and then in her workplace, if she can pump, all she needs is a small room to herself with perhaps a small refrigerator and she can continue to breastfeed that baby.

Hostess: And very quickly, ideally how long should you do it? I did it for six months.

Dr. Reichman: We want six months exclusively. If possible, then add on a supplement for a year, and we encourage … the American Academy of Pediatrics encourages breastfeeding for two years.

Hostess: Wow. Yes. But when they can ask for it, they are too old. Right?

Dr. Reichman: Well. "Mommy. Mommy."

Hostess: I don't know. That kind of ~~erazed~~ [freaks] me out. All right. Judith, thank you very much.

五、补充阅读

1）Gillies, A. (2009). *Note-taking for Consecutive Interpreting: A Short Course*. Shanghai: Shanghai Foreign Language Education Press.

2）雷天放，陈菁. 口译教程 [M]. 上海：上海外语教育出版社，2006.

3）仲伟合，王斌华. 基础口译 [M]. 北京：外语教学与研究出版社，2009.

第8章 ▶ 记大意之间的联系

一、技能解说

1）逻辑连接词体现了大意之间的逻辑联系，如and、but、however、because、therefore等。它们反映了笔记过程中的思考过程，不仅体现讲话人的思路，也有利于听众的理解。

2）口译所依赖的短时记忆容量是有限的，国际公认的记忆容量是7个信息单位左右。口译中，如果把段落意思分成几个有意义的组块，利用逻辑连接词联系在一起，会更容易记住。

3）听的同时对信息进行分析加工，将分析的结果，即大意之间的联系，通过恰当的方式用笔记记录下来。表达的时候笔记主要起提示作用，绝对不能念笔记。

4）无论讲话长短，译员要以大脑记忆为主，以笔记为辅。先分析，再笔记。

听讲话的时候不要急于记笔记，因为如果只记一些词汇，在表达的时候用处不大。如果听完讲话根本没有理解，甚至因为记录影响了对讲话的理解，表达的时候就会语无伦次，不知所云，即使能说出几个词汇，也无法保证信息的交流。相反，如果能借助自己的认知知识理解和把握整体意义，即使有个别不认识的词汇也不会影响整个信息，反而可能会在交际环境中被正确地理解（刘和平，2009，p. 86）。

5）重点记语段开始和结尾的信息。

✓ 语段开头通常都包含若干称谓，很可能贯穿始终，最好不要记漏或记错，名字的发音也最好提早确认。

✓ 如果语段较长，可以在中间适当回忆开头的信息。

✓ 记录结尾时要做到"有始有终"。语段结束后的2~5秒、译员开口翻译之前，一定抓住这几秒完成最后一句的笔记，让自己的译语"有头有尾"。

二、训练方法

● 听演讲材料、看电视或听广播，按照口译笔记要求进行记录；记关键词，尤其记开头结尾的笔记；注意补充句间的逻辑连接词。可以同学间相互检查，体会笔记的作用。

● 结合上周内容，看笔记的结构和所记的内容是否合理、是否可用。如果发现问题，应分析其原因，并进行改进。

● 摸索个人记录的方法和策略，尤其应该体会先听后写的口译笔记原则。

三、练习案例点评

———————————————— 案例1 ————————————————

源　　语：But "we must not underestimate the impact of the crisis on China's economy," he said, while reporting to the fifth session of the Standing Committee of the National People's Congress, or NPC.

Despite the impact of the global financial crisis, Zhou said, "We should recognize that the overall economic condition is good; our financial institutions are generally strong; with increased profit-making and risk-fending abilities, market liquidity on the whole is ample and our financial system is sound and safe."

Moreover, continuing urbanization and industrialization, which generate huge investment demand, as well as the large domestic market and low-cost labor, mean the basic economic growth track will not deviate much, he said.

学生译语："但是我们不能低估此次危机对中国经济的影响。"周在全国人大常委会第五次会议上汇报称。虽然受到全球金融危机的影响，但是我们也要认识到，中国经济总体态势良好，金融机构强健，金融系统稳健安全，并且因为城镇化和工业化，投资需求大，内需市场大，劳动力价格低，经济增长总趋势不会有太大变化。

📋 点评

1）总体还不错，大意都译出来了，但有部分细节遗漏。
2）中文译语不够地道。比如，译语中的"但是"太多。中文是意合语言，不需要"但是"就能体现句间逻辑关系。"周在全国人大常委会第五次会议上汇报称"这句也不太符合中文习惯。英文可以用姓代指某个人，中文多用"头衔+全名"。
3）漏译了with increased profit-making and risk-fending abilities, market liquidity on the whole is ample这部分信息。推测可能是译前准备不足，fending和liquidity都是金融术语，如果没听懂很容易导致大面积漏译。
4）要注意句间逻辑连接词。moreover后的内容明显是另外一点，应该另起一句，译语会更清楚。

教师评分：85。

案例2

源　语： At the NPC session yesterday, Wu Xiaoling, vice-chairwoman of the Financial and Economic (Affairs) Committee, sounded a cautionary note when responding to Zhou's report.

She warned that in the next two or three years, China could face more difficult times than during the 1997–1998 Asian financial crisis.

Wu said the current situation is grimmer than a decade ago because the proportion of the country's exports to GDP is higher while the problem of overcapacity could lead to reduced investment in such sectors as steel and electricity generation.

The real estate bubble has taken housing out of the reach of many while car sales meet the bottleneck of high oil prices and environmental constraints, she said.

"It is challenging to boost economic growth by encouraging people to spend," she said. "We should get prepared for difficulties."

学生译语： 中国的经济部女部长在人民代表大会上发表了这样的一段话。中国在两到三年后遇到的困境将会比在1997年至1998年亚洲金融危机面临的困难要更多、更大。且中国现在形势比十年前还要更加令人忧心，这是因为中国出口占GDP的占额正在不断地增加。这会使得中国在某些区域如电力生产、钢铁生产的投资比例下降。此外房价不断攀升，已经超出许多人的能力之外，油价也不断地攀升，以及受到其他的一些经济限制。此外，胡称中国正面临着很大的挑战，因为要通过刺激消费来刺激经济的增长，中国需要为即将到来的困难做好准备。

点评

1）大意基本完整：先是警告，跟着是三个论据，最后是直接引用。但细节方面有待提高。

2）存在人名和头衔表达不准确的情况，开头没记住时任财政经济委员会副主任委员的姓名，后面再次出现时又将人物姓氏误译为"胡"。记忆人名时，可以用姓氏来代替；头衔如果在听的时候不好确定，可以先记下部门或机构的首字母缩写来应对。

3）"发表了这样的一段话"不符合新闻报道的话语特点，应该注意根据源语的语境选择合适的表达风格。

4）sounded a cautionary note漏译。

5）"占GDP的占额"有语病。前面已经有"占"，"占额"改成"份额"

比较好。听时简记的关键词不适合直接搬进译语，应当边说边想边改口，重新组织语言。overcapacity漏译。

6）没有理解real estate bubble的含义，根据语境处理为"房价攀升"不够准确，应直译为"房地产泡沫"。car sales meet the bottleneck of high oil prices and environmental constraints译为"油价也不断地攀升，以及受到其他的一些经济限制"，漏译信息较多，什么限制什么的关系理解有误，推测可能是因为bottleneck这个表达没听懂。

7）最后一句的逻辑关系和源语不一致。挑战和鼓励消费的关系不是"因为"，应调整语序，译为"通过鼓励人们消费而促进经济增长并非易事"。

教师评分：82。

四、篇章练习

生词表

英文	中文
U.S. Census Bureau	美国人口调查局
Vatican City	梵蒂冈
non-communicable	非传染性的
risk-fending	规避风险的
market liquidity	市场流动性
reserve requirement ratio	存款准备金率

1）World population review

练习说明：

1. This is a report on world population in 2019 by an organization posted on a technology community platform. Brainstorm before listening: Do you know how the current world population is distributed across continents, countries, cities, etc.? What might have contributed to the population increase or decrease?

2. The report is divided into five segments. Take notes and interpret at each stop signal, and record your interpretation.

3. After interpreting,

   1) review your recording for quality: Does your interpretation contain any language

fillers, pauses longer than three seconds, disorganized information, or unidiomatic expressions?

2) reflect upon your notes. What strategies did you use for STM and note-taking respectively? Did you get the correct numbers? If not, what caused the errors and how to improve? Discuss your notes and compare them with those of your peers.

The current U.S. Census Bureau world population estimate in June 2019 shows that the current global population is 7,577,130,400 people on Earth, which far exceeds the world population of 7.2 billion from 2015. Our own estimate based on UN data shows the world's population surpassing 7.7 billion.

China is the most populous country in the world with a population exceeding 1.4 billion. It is one of just two countries with a population of more than 1 billion, with India being the second. As of 2018, India has a population of over 1.355 billion people, and its population growth is expected to continue through at least 2050. By the year 2030, the country of India is expected to become the most populous country in the world. This is because India's population will grow, while China is projected to see a loss in population.

The next 11 countries that are the most populous in the world each have populations exceeding 100 million. These include the United States, Indonesia, Brazil, Pakistan, Nigeria, Bangladesh, Russia, Mexico, Japan, Ethiopia, and the Philippines. Of these nations, all are expected to continue to grow except Russia and Japan, which will see their populations drop by 2030 before falling again significantly by 2050.

Many other nations have populations of at least one million, while there are also countries that have just thousands. The smallest population in the world can be found in Vatican City, where only 801 people reside.

In 2018, the world's population growth rate was 1.12 percent. Every five years since the 1970s, the population growth rate has continued to fall. The world's population is expected to continue to grow larger but at a much slower pace. By 2030, the population will exceed eight billion. In 2040, this number will grow to more than nine billion. In 2055, the number will rise to over 10 billion, and another billion people won't be added until near the end of the century. The current annual population growth estimates from the United Nations are in the millions — estimating that over 80 million new lives are added each year.

This population growth will be significantly impacted by nine specific countries which are situated to contribute to the population growth more quickly than other nations. These nations include the Democratic Republic of the Congo, Ethiopia, India, Indonesia, Nigeria, Pakistan, Uganda, the United Republic of Tanzania, and the United States of America. Particularly of interest, India is on track to overtake China's position as the most populous country by the year 2030. Additionally, multiple nations within Africa are expected to double their populations before fertility rates begin to slow entirely.

Global life expectancy has also improved in recent years, increasing the overall population life expectancy at birth to just over 70 years of age. The projected global life expectancy is only expected to continue to improve — reaching nearly 77 years of age by the year 2050. Significant factors impacting the data on life expectancy include the projections of the ability to reduce AIDS/HIV impact, as well as reducing the rates of infectious and non-communicable diseases.

Population aging has a massive impact on the ability of the population to maintain what is called a support ratio. One key finding from 2017 is that the majority of the world is going to face considerable growth in the 60 plus age bracket. This will put enormous strain on the younger age groups as the elderly population is becoming so vast without the number of births to maintain a healthy support ratio.

2）China coping with the global financial crisis

练习说明：

1. This is a news report about the impact of the 2008 global financial crisis on China.
2. The report is divided into six segments. Take notes and interpret the message at each stop signal, and record your interpretation. Here's a tip for you: Given that many authoritative remarks are cited to support opinions in this news report, it is important to figure out "who says what to support what," especially when multiple resources are cited all at once.
3. After interpreting,
    1) review your recording for quality: Does your interpretation contain any language fillers, pauses longer than three seconds, disorganized information, or unidiomatic expressions?
    2) reflect upon your notes. What did you note down and how did you do it? Which did you rely on more in interpreting, STM, or your notes? Which was more helpful for interpreting this news report, and why?

The fundamentals of the Chinese economy remain sound and the country can cope with the challenges posed by the worsening global financial crisis, central bank governor Zhou Xiaochuan told legislators yesterday.

But "we must not underestimate the impact of the crisis on China's economy," he said, while reporting to the fifth session of the Standing Committee of the National People's Congress, or NPC.

Despite the impact of the global financial crisis, Zhou said, "We should recognize that the overall economic condition is good; our financial institutions are generally strong; with increased profit-making and risk-fending abilities, market liquidity on the whole is ample and our financial system is sound and safe."

Moreover, continuing urbanization and industrialization, which generate huge investment demand, as well as the large domestic market and low-cost labor, mean the basic economic growth track will not deviate much, he said.

Lin Yifu, senior vice-president and chief economist of the World Bank, also said the impact of the global financial crisis on China would be "limited." In the era of globalization, no place is a safe haven, but China's economic condition is one of the best compared with others, he said at Peking University on Saturday.

China's GDP growth slowed to nine percent in the third quarter from 10.1 percent in the second. As the global economy is expected to slow, China's growth may weaken further, although it may avoid a hard landing, economists said.

At the NPC session yesterday, Wu Xiaoling, vice-chairwoman of the Financial and Economic (Affairs) Committee, sounded a cautionary note when responding to Zhou's report.

She warned that in the next two or three years, China could face more difficult times than during the 1997–1998 Asian financial crisis.

Wu said the current situation is grimmer than a decade ago because the proportion of the country's exports to GDP is higher while the problem of overcapacity could lead to reduced investment in such sectors as steel and electricity generation.

The real estate bubble has taken housing out of the reach of many while car sales meet the bottleneck of high oil prices and environmental constraints, she said.

"It is challenging to boost economic growth by encouraging people to spend," she said. "We should get prepared for difficulties."

The country has taken a slew of monetary and fiscal measures recently to boost growth, including two cuts in interest rates and banks' reserve requirement ratio, a proportion that money lenders must hold in reserve. Analysts said more policy relaxations could be in the offing if needed.

"If there are signs of further economic weakening and sapping investor confidence, policymakers may further cut interest rates or the bank reserve requirement," said Ma Ming, economist with the Beijing Institute of Technology.

But Wu — pointing out lessons to be learned from the U.S. economy — warned that in the long term, it is not advisable to keep money costs low to stimulate the economy. Economists agree that low interest rates in the U.S. during the past decade have sown the seeds for today's financial crisis.

Zhou also said that inflation could rebound in the coming months and the central bank would keep a close eye on consumer prices. In September, inflation eased to 4.6 percent from a peak of 8.7 percent in February.

3）An open letter from a U.S. college to Chinese students in response to COVID-19

练习说明：

1. This is an open letter from a U.S. college to its Chinese students and their families in response to COVID-19. Before you listen, try to predict the outline of the content and articulate it in your own words, and think of terms about COVID-19.

2. The material is divided into four segments. Interpret the message at each stop signal and record your interpretation.

3. After interpreting,
   1) review your recording for quality: Does your interpretation contain any language fillers, pauses longer than three seconds, disorganized information, or unidiomatic expressions?
   2) reflect upon your notes. Did you take notes in a proper form? How did you note down the main ideas and the links between them? Did your notes serve as a backup of your STM?

Dear Students and Families,

Warm greetings from California. We are writing with an update about how our college is responding to the rapidly-changing COVID-19 pandemic. Please rest assured that we are following state and local guidelines, which are more stringent than (those of) the U.S. as a whole. Our administration responded early and proactively, before official guidelines were published, with several important measures.

When the decision was made to move all courses to remote instruction, we realized the importance of acting decisively to cause as little disruption as possible, especially with the interests of our international student population in mind. This was not a decision we made lightly, but at the forefront of our decision was the health and well-being of our community.

By committing immediately to offering all courses remotely for the rest of the semester, we ensured that students had the chance to decide for themselves where they wanted to be located. While many students opted to stay in our small and friendly city, others sought the comfort of family and friends, either elsewhere in the United States or back home.

We took great care to offer faculty training and technical assistance to successfully transition their classes and we are fully committed to the continuity of studies for all students, held to the same outstanding standards our college is known for. All faculty and staff are working remotely and are available to students via video calls, phone calls, and emails. Staff are continuing to offer excellent services in innovative ways, including career advising, health and wellness support, and library services. The administration meets several times a day to review new developments, and as always, the guiding light in all decisions is the safety and health of our students and the community.

Our college prides itself on the diversity of its population — with students, staff, and faculty from all over the world. That is at the heart of who we are and is what makes learning here such a rich and rewarding experience.

If you would like to stay up-to-date on our response to the outbreak, you're welcome to follow us on WeChat, Weibo or visit our COVID-19 website. Thank you.

五、补充阅读

1）Gillies, A. (2009). *Note-taking for Consecutive Interpreting: A Short Course*. Shanghai: Shanghai Foreign Language Education Press.

2）雷天放，陈菁. 口译教程 [M]. 上海：上海外语教育出版社，2006.

3）刘敏华. 逐步口译与笔记：理论、实践与教学 [M]. 台北：书林出版有限公司，2008.

第9章 ▶ 笔记符号

一、技能解说

1）译员的笔记很有个性，别人几乎无法使用，即使是该笔记的作者，如果不是当时使用，也不一定有保存的意义（刘和平，2009，p. 96）。笔记记录的内容、效果等还会受到讲话内容的难度、长度，以及讲话人的口音等因素的影响。

2）经验丰富的职业译员一般都拥有一套相对固定、自成体系的个人笔记符号，使用时可不假思索，运用自如。口译初学者虽然知道笔记原则和手段，但由于缺乏一个从感性到理性的"顿悟"过程，又没有熟练的操作经验，需花费很多精力和时间选择笔记记录的信息、语言及符号，操作受相关机制的高度控制，过程长却效率低。

可以通过练习，逐步发展和优化个人笔记方法：

- ✓ 在笔记中，使用个人熟悉且容易辨认的数学、化学、物理、音乐单位或符号和其他符号、箭头、线条等表达意义。
- ✓ 注意掌握国际和国内组织及重要机构的常见缩略词，比如NGO、G8、APEC、CPPCC等。
- ✓ 逐渐积累自己习惯使用和容易辨识的缩写词，要简明、易辨认，并保持一致。
- ✓ 可根据这样的笔记书写原则发展出个人笔记方法：少写多划，少字多意，少横多竖，快速书写，明确结束（林超伦，2004，p. 3-7）。

3）数字笔记原则：

- ✓ 数字笔记一定要与其所附的相关信息（如单位等）结合；
- ✓ 数字笔记的翻译同样需要借助交际语境；
- ✓ 数字与其相关的信息产生笔记或记忆冲突时，信息通常优先。

二、训练方法

- 回忆无笔记训练时分析之后存在脑中的"标签"，它们能否变成笔记？听同样一段话，体会无笔记译与有笔记译的区别。
- 小组讨论和交流，听演讲材料、看电视或听广播的访谈类节目，边听边记笔记，体会笔记的原则和方法。每位同学都做笔记和口译后，结合译语讨论笔记，互相学习和借鉴。
- 大量练习带数字的段落，体会记忆数字和信息的技巧；找出自己在数字翻译中的主要弱点，有针对性地加强训练。

三、练习案例点评

—————— 案例1 ——————

源　语： Multitasking is something that we all do. It isn't always a problem. Some people are truly better at multitasking than others — people with small children. If your main job is looking after small children, it's really difficult to do without being a good multitasker. And in 2022, fathers may also be the main carer for their children — and handle it really well. What about that old statement that sometimes people make — "Women are better at multitasking"? Have you heard that? If I'm being really contentious here, there is some research which suggests that women are better at multitasking!

学生译语： 我们经常会多线程工作，或者说一心多用。通常来说这种工作方式并不是一个问题。有人更擅长多线程工作，这种擅长程度比他人更强。特别是那些有小孩的人，如果不擅长多线程工作的话，很可能会对小孩照顾不周。一些爸爸照顾小孩子的时候就会经常多线程工作且表现良好。那么人们是怎么做到多线程工作的呢？一般来说，女性更擅长一心多用，这也是有研究证明的。

📋 点评

1）该译语抓住了部分细节信息，但对总体逻辑的把握稍有欠缺，有不必要增译。此外应注意把握讲话的语气。

2）multitasking先是译为"多线程工作"，后又解释为"一心多用"，两者混用，可能给听众造成理解障碍。应该保持译语前后一致。

3）"有人更擅长多线程工作，这种擅长程度比他人更强"意思准确，但听起来生硬，有翻译腔。

4）"特别是那些有小孩的人，如果不擅长多线程工作的话，很可能会对小孩照顾不周"总体没有偏离原意，但没有强调原文中的信息if your main job is looking after small children。

5）"一些爸爸照顾小孩子的时候就会经常多线程工作且表现良好"缺乏对"2022"这个年代背景信息的强调，属于漏译。

教师评分：80。

源　　语： What's clear from that research is that the requirement to multitask slows anyone's performance down significantly. And perhaps in the workplace, if multitasking is something that's required of you, imposed upon you — and if the expectation is high, it's more of a problem.

Other research supports the idea that multitasking reduces your productivity! Too much multitasking affects your efficiency, your productivity. You do less overall. If you're working on a project which needs your focus, your concentration, but you're constantly interrupted by telephone calls or people asking for your help, or lots of meetings, it may be difficult to make progress or feel as though you're achieving anything.

学生译语： 研究表明，如果有人需要去进行多任……多项任务处理的话，这会严重地影响他的生产效率。如果是在一项工作当中，你被迫要去同时处理多项的事情，在这个过程当中，你还要处理好自己手头的事情，而且别人对你的期待还比较高的话，多项任务处理是会严重地降低你的生产效率。如果你在一个工作当中，你需要去处理一项任务，你就需要去集中于这项任务，但是如果在这个过程当中有电话源源不断地打进来，然后也有人不断地寻求你的帮助，或者是你需要开很多的会议，那么你就无法很好地去解决你需要去做的这个事情，那就会使你的获得感减少。总之多项处理会让你……总的会让你效率总的……总体变得更低。

📖 **点评**

1）总体意思比较准确，但自我重复和改口比较多，影响理解。另外，还存在一些细节问题。

2）人称代词使用冗余，尤其是过多使用"你"。第三人称和第二人称同时使用会有些混乱。中文不需要过多人称代词，在上下文中其意自明，且言简意赅。

3）有些概念没有表达清楚，如in the workplace是泛指在工作中，而不是具体指一项工作。feel as though you're achieving anything更多是描述"成就感"，而非"获得感"。

4）"如果是在一项工作当中，你被迫要去同时处理多项的事情，在这个过程当中，你还要处理好自己手头的事情，而且别人对你的期待还比较高的话，多项任务处理是会严重地降低你的生产效率"这句话的信息逻辑有错误。"在这个过程当中，你还要处理好自己手头的事情"是多余的；"多项任务处理是会严重地降低你的生产效率"

是下一句的内容，和本句前半句不构成因果关系，此处应该译为
"多项任务处理会更成问题"或"多项任务处理会造成问题叠加"。

5）信息点出现的先后顺序也有些混乱，如"总之多项处理会让你……
总的会让你效率总的……总体变得更低"应该在前一句出现；且此
处只译了efficiency，漏译了productivity。

教师评分：85。

四、篇章练习

生词表

英文	中文
multitasking	多重任务处理，同时做数件事情
swap	交换，切换
outperform	胜过，做得比……更好
chunk	组块
overhead	间接费用，（企业的）经常性开支
prioritize	划分优先顺序，优先安排
Czech Republic	捷克共和国
United Parcel Service, Inc., UPS	美国联合包裹运送服务公司
Yosemite	约塞米蒂国家公园
Sierra Nevada Mountains	内华达山脉（位于美国加利福尼亚州东部）
Half Dome	半圆顶巨岩
Mariposa Grove	马里波萨谷巨杉林
sequoia	红杉
granite	花岗岩
El Capitan	埃尔卡皮坦巨岩，酋长岩
Miwok	米沃克人（北美印第安人民族）

1）Tackling multitasking to avoid workplace stress

练习说明：

1. This is a talk titled "Stress and How to Avoid It." Brainstorm before listening: Have you
heard of "multitasking"? Can you provide some tips for managing workplace stress?
Please give some examples.

2. The talk is divided into 13 segments. Please take notes and interpret. Record your interpretation at each stop signal.
3. After interpreting,
   1) review your recording for quality: Did you get the correct message? Does your interpretation contain any language fillers, pauses longer than three seconds, disorganized information, or unidiomatic expressions?
   2) think about the following questions: Did you feel struggled and pay extra cognitive efforts when you took notes? How did your notes contribute to or hinder your interpretation, and why? Discuss better ways of note-taking with your peers.

Workplace stress seems to have increased massively during the pandemic. And there is evidence that we're all under greater pressure to multitask than ever before, even if you're not at work — and certainly if you are at home looking after children — then multitasking is a pressure for you too. Today then, I'm going to look at why and how multitasking can be a bad thing, especially at work, and what you can do about it. And I've got some really important advice specially for you.

Multitasking is something that we all do. It isn't always a problem. Some people are truly better at multitasking than others — people with small children. If your main job is looking after small children, it's really difficult to do without being a good multitasker. And in 2022, fathers may also be the main carer for their children — and handle it really well. What about that old statement that sometimes people make — "Women are better at multitasking"? Have you heard that? If I'm being really contentious here, there is some research which suggests that women are better at multitasking!

A study in 2013 published by the journal *BMC Psychology* found that swapping from task to task wasn't great for anybody, but that men suffered the effects more. Men took longer to adjust and become productive at a new task than women did. This research took 120 men and 120 women and gave them a computerized test, which meant swapping between activities.

Men's and women's performance was about the same, if they stayed on the same task. But when the test made them swap between tasks, it became clear that women slightly outperformed men. Women were 69 percent slower when multitasking and men were 77 percent slower. It doesn't sound like that much of a difference, but it would make a difference over time.

What's clear from that research is that the requirement to multitask slows anyone's performance down significantly. And perhaps in the workplace, if multitasking is something that's required of you, imposed upon you — and if the expectation is high, it's more of a problem.

Other research supports the idea that multitasking reduces your productivity! Too much multitasking affects your efficiency, your productivity. You do less overall. If you're working on a project which needs your focus, your concentration, but you're constantly interrupted by telephone calls or people asking for your help, or lots of meetings, it may be difficult to make progress or feel as though you're achieving anything.

Job satisfaction — that means "how positive you feel about your job" — and motivation can be affected too.

Sometimes multitasking is a problem in a workplace because you have to answer to a different boss for each different task, each different part of your work. The problem here may be that nobody but you knows just how much work you have.

Nobody else can see the pressure that you're under overall. Your bosses may only know or care about the work you do for them. This is a dangerous situation from the point of view of your stress level. Workers can be particularly vulnerable if they find themselves in this situation.

One of the questions I always ask my clients: "How many hours a week do you work?" If you're working over 50 hours a week for a long period of time, that will affect your physical and your mental health.

Multitasking makes each task more difficult because we rely to a point on our short-term memory to carry out a task. We have long-term memory, where we can store unlimited amounts of information fairly permanently — forever, if you like — if we learn it well. But our short-term memory, which we use for tasks, has limited storage. So if we're constantly multitasking, we're asking a lot of our short-term memory. We're trying to hold lots of pieces of information about lots of different tasks in our short-term memory, so we don't perform as well — it doesn't work!

There's also evidence that constantly swapping between tasks affects our capacity to concentrate, our ability to focus. If you think about the effects of social media, it's all designed to capture our attention, but then nothing holds our attention for very long. So our brains become used to only maintaining a focus for a short period of time, rather than prolonged periods of deep focus. That's not good then.

How do we solve this problem of being required to multitask? Maybe first of all, some reflection on how much multitasking you do, what amount of multitasking is required of you, and why. Is it necessary? If it is, then you might organize your work into "chunks." If you break your work into "chunks," it means that you do a significant amount of work on the same task before moving on to a different task. This will help maximize your productivity when you have several tasks going on and it helps to maintain your focus. In effect, the more "task-swapping" you do, the worse it is.

So try to reduce the number of times a day that you swap from one task to another. Computers are great at multitasking. Human beings? Not so much! There's an "overhead" each time we "task-swap." It takes time for us to refocus and arrive at concentrating on the new task.

You could prioritize your tasks for the month, the week, or the day. It means that you don't lose sight of what's most important when you're working.

This will make sure that you're working on the most important things. Sometimes there are "quick wins" as we say — small tasks that you prioritize, just to get something done, something finished. That's good for your motivation.

And minimize the number of times a day that you check messages, especially your work email. Generally, if people email you, they're not expecting an answer straight away. Perhaps think of reserving some time at the beginning and again at the end of your working day just to check your email.

Constantly checking your email is not usually necessary and it wastes time. The same with your mobile phone! It interferes with your concentration and focus. Those messages will wait! Just check it occasionally!

2）Beginnings of speeches

练习说明:

1. There are two excerpts taken from the beginnings of two speeches given at Boao Forum for Asia. Brainstorm before listening: Who are the speakers and the audience of these speeches? What kind of information might be difficult to interpret?
2. Each of the speech excerpts is divided into two segments. Record your interpretation at each stop signal.
3. After interpreting,
   1) review your recording for quality: Does your interpretation contain any language fillers, pauses longer than three seconds, disorganized information, or unidiomatic expressions?
   2) think about the following questions: How do you assess your interpretation? Why was it successful or why not? Did you find your notes helpful? Share your assessment with your peers.

Excerpt 1

Your Excellency Mr. Vaclav Klaus, President of Czech Republic,

Mr. President David Abney, President of UPS International,

Your Excellency Ambassador Wu Jianmin, President of China Foreign Affairs University,

Honorable guests,

Friends,

Ladies and gentlemen,

I am very pleased to have the opportunity to address this CEO Summit. This is a great honor for me and I would like to thank you for this invitation.

At the official opening of this conference yesterday I explained that win-win situations for regions and companies arise, when both sides benefit from a partnership with a long-term scope. This happens through both sides bundling their strengths and know-how.

Today I would like to carry these aspects somewhat further. My core message here is the following: When the inherent strengths on individual markets and inherent strengths of companies operating there are bundled, the result is even more than the sum of the individual capabilities. The applicable equation here is 1+1=3 or even more, and that is a win-win situation for both sides.

Excerpt 2

Your Excellencies,

Distinguished members of the Boao Forum,

Dear colleagues,

Ladies and gentlemen,

First, before I begin my keynote speech, I would like to convey a congratulatory message on the occasion of this year's Boao Forum from His Excellency Mr. Goh Kun, Prime Minister and Acting President of the Republic of Korea.

I shall read the message on his behalf: "I would like to extend my sincere congratulations to you on the occasion of the 2004 Annual Conference of the Boao Forum for Asia. I would also like to convey my deepest appreciation to all those who have worked tirelessly for the success of the Forum. By providing the vision and practical guidance, the Boao Forum will play a central role for greater development and cooperation in Asia. I hope that, through this occasion, we will demonstrate to the rest of the world an Asia that is truly open to the world and in search for (of a) win-win (solution). Thank you."

It is truly a great honor to stand here today, among the leaders of our region. I would like to express my deepest gratitude to everyone who helped to organize this year's forum.

3）Endings of speeches

练习说明：

1. There are three excerpts taken from the concluding parts of three speeches given at Boao Forum for Asia. Brainstorm before listening: What might be covered at the end of these speeches?
2. Interpret the message at each stop signal and record your interpretation.
3. After interpreting,
   1) review your recording for quality: Did you get the correct message? Does your interpretation contain any language fillers, pauses longer than three seconds, disorganized information, or unidiomatic expressions?
   2) think about the following questions: How do you assess your interpretation? Why was it successful or why not? Did you find your notes helpful? Share your assessment with your peers.

Excerpt 1

Successful economic locations combine their inherent strengths with inherent strengths of international corporations engaged in the region. And then the equation that I mentioned at the beginning will prove its validity: One plus one will not only result in two, but in three, four, and even more. Thank you.

Excerpt 2

I know I have suggested a lot of things which I cannot do by myself. I hope I have attracted the attention of the government departments. We need to push one another at the government level in order to develop a cooperative and interactive Asian film and TV industry. It will take a long time, and there will be struggles. But I know we will succeed. As Chairman Mao said, "So many deeds cry out to be done, and always urgently; the world rolls on, time ~~passed~~ (presses)." I hope we can "seize the day, seize the hour," and to see this day soon, participate in this ideal. Thank you.

Excerpt 3

Mr. Chairman Morris Chang,
Distinguished guests,

Whichever way we are to look at it, this is going to be the Asian century. I am sure that like myself, all of you would consider yourselves fortunate to be part of this. We are the participants, we are the drivers, and we are the beneficiaries. As we stand at the cusp of this wonderful opportunity, we must ensure that as responsible participants in this process, we all take, and help implement the right decisions that would eventually deliver on the promised opportunity that the environment offers us today. Thank you.

4）Yosemite National Park

练习说明：

1. This is a talk about Yosemite National Park. It is one of the most beautiful national parks in the U.S., high in the Sierra Nevada Mountains of the western state of California. Brainstorm before listening: What do you know about Yosemite? Do you know its history? Were you the speaker, how would you introduce this scenic spot to your audience, and how would you organize your talk?

2. The talk is divided into 10 segments. Interpret the message at each stop signal and record your interpretation.

3. After interpreting,
   1) review your recording for quality: Did you get the correct message? Does your interpretation contain any language fillers, pauses longer than three seconds, disorganized information, or unidiomatic expressions?
   2) think about the following questions:
      - Did you use any symbols or signs in your notes? Did you interpret the numbers and their corresponding information correctly? Did your notes serve as a backup of your STM?
      - What did you find difficult when interpreting a descriptive speech as such?

Yosemite National Park is a place of extremes. It has high mountains. It has valleys formed by ancient ice that cut deep into the Earth millions of years ago. Water from high in the mountains falls in many places to the green valley far below. There are 13 beautiful waterfalls in Yosemite Valley. One of these waterfalls, Yosemite Falls, is the fifth highest on Earth.

Up in the mountains are clear lakes, quick-moving small rivers, and huge formations of rock. One huge rock is called Half Dome. It rises about 2,700 meters into the air.

Yosemite has a beautiful slow-moving river and large grassy areas where you can see wild animals. More than 60 kinds of animals live in the park. Deer are very common. You can see them almost everywhere. They have little fear of humans. You might even see a large black bear.

You can also see 200 different kinds of birds.

In a place called the Mariposa Grove, visitors can see some of the largest, tallest, and oldest living things on Earth. These are the giant sequoia trees. One of these trees is called Grizzly Giant. It is more than 1,800 years old. One tree is almost 90 meters tall. Another is more than 10 meters around. The huge old trees can make you feel very, very small.

The story of the Sierra Nevada Mountains and the area that is Yosemite National Park begins [began] about 500 million years ago. The area then was at the bottom of an ancient sea.

Scientists believe strong earthquakes forced the bottom of the sea to rise above the water. After millions of years, it was pushed up into the air to form land and mountains, at the same time, hot liquid rock from deep in the Earth pushed to the surface. This liquid rock slowly cooled. This cooling liquid formed a very hard rock known as granite.

Many centuries of rain caused huge rivers to move violently through this area. Over time, these rivers cut deep into the new mountains. During the great Ice Age, millions of tons of ice cut and shaped the cooled granite to form giant rocks. Millions of years later these would become the giant rocks called Half Dome and El Capitan in Yosemite Park.

Humans have lived in the area of Yosemite for more than 4,000 years. The first people who lived there were hunters. Most were members of a tribe of Native Americans called the Miwok. They lived in Yosemite Valley near the river.

During the extremely cold winters, these people would move to lower, warmer areas. They would return when the winter months had passed.

The first white Americans may have been hunters looking for fur animals. A famous American hunter and explorer named Joseph Walker passed through the area in the 1830s. He reported about the huge rock formations and said there was no way to reach the valley below.

Citizens who had formed a military group were the first real modern explorers of the valley. They were at war with the local Indians and came into the valley. The white soldiers called the Indians "Yosemites." The valley was named for the Indian tribe. Soon, reports of its great natural beauty were sent all the way back to Washington, D.C.

In 1864, a United States senator called for legislation to give the Yosemite Valley to the state of California as a public park. The legislation said the valley should be preserved and protected. President Abraham Lincoln signed the bill after Congress approved it.

This event was extremely important in the history of the United States. It was the first time that a government had approved a law to preserve and protect land because of its great beauty. The land was to be kept for the public to enjoy. Yosemite became the first state park. It was the first real park in the world. In 1890, it became a national park. The National Park Service is responsible for the park today. It is preserved and protected for all people to enjoy.

No major roads lead to Yosemite National Park. Visitors must leave the highways and drive their cars over smaller roads. Yosemite is about 320 kilometers east of San Francisco. It is deep in the Sierra Nevada Mountains. The roads leading to the park pass over lower parts of the huge mountains. Then the road goes lower and lower into the area of the park called Yosemite Valley.

Visitors can stay in different kinds of places in Yosemite Park. Several beautiful old hotels have been built on the property. Some are very costly. Others cost less. Many people bring temporary cloth homes called tents. It costs only a few dollars a day to place a tent in the approved areas.

Visitors can walk through many areas in the beautiful valley and the mountains. These walking paths are called trails. The National Park Service has improved more than 1,100 kilometers of trails. It is fun to explore these trails. Some take only a few minutes to walk. Others can take several days to complete.

People come from all over the world to climb one of the huge rock formations at Yosemite. The most famous of these is called El Capitan. People who climb it call it "El Cap." Climbing El Cap is only for experts. This activity is called "hard rock climbing." It is extremely difficult and can be very dangerous.

A climber must have expert skill and great strength. The climb is straight up the face of a rock wall. Experts say it can take about three days to climb to the top of El Cap. The climbing is very slow.

Climbers must look for cracks in the rock. They place their hands and feet in the cracks and then work their way up. They also use ropes and special equipment. From the bottom of the valley to the top of El Cap is about 1,100 meters.

In the summer months, Yosemite Park is filled with visitors. Large buses bring people from San Francisco to spend the day.

They leave San Francisco very early in the morning and arrive back late at night. They drive from one place to another to see Yosemite. Other visitors come by car.

Some even come by bicycle. Some visit for just a few hours. Others take several days or weeks to enjoy the park. Many visitors come to Yosemite again and again. About four million people visit the park every year.

In the winter, heavy snow falls in the Sierra Nevada Mountains and Yosemite. The snow usually begins to fall in the month of November. Heavy snow forces some of the roads into Yosemite to close during the winter months. The National Park Service works hard to keep most of the roads open.

Drivers must use special care because of ice and snow on the roads. They enjoy a special beauty never seen by the summer visitors. Many winter visitors come to Yosemite to spend their time skiing at Badger Pass. Badger Ski Area is the oldest in California. It has a ski school for those who want to learn the exciting sport.

Many visitors come to enjoy the park with its heavy coat of winter snow. In some areas the snow is many meters deep. Some of the tall mountains keep their snow until the last hot days of summer.

Whenever visitors come to Yosemite, they experience great natural beauty. A visit to the park provides lasting memories of what nature has produced. Most people who come to Yosemite usually bring a camera. They take many pictures of the huge rocks, the beautiful Yosemite Valley, the waterfalls, and the giant trees.

But you do not really need a photograph to remember its great natural beauty. Yosemite will leave its image in your memory forever.

五、补充阅读

1）Gillies, A. (2009). *Note-taking for Consecutive Interpreting: A Short Course*. Shanghai: Shanghai Foreign Language Education Press.

2）林超伦. 实战口译 [M]. 北京：外语教学与研究出版社，2004.

3）刘敏华. 逐步口译与笔记：理论、实践与教学 [M]. 台北：书林出版有限公司，2008.

4）吴钟明. 英语口译笔记法实战指导 [M]. 武汉：武汉大学出版社，2005.

第**10**章 ▶ 笔记与表达

一、技能解说

1）译员笔记的并不是独立的符号或数字，而是借助脑记（即短期记忆）将这些符号或数字同大脑中经过分析加工的内容融合在一起。译员一见到某个符号时便会迅速联想或回忆起刚刚听到的内容，实现记忆提取（retrieval）。

2）听的时候，笔记可以帮助集中精神和减轻记忆负担；表达的时候，笔记可以帮助回忆起相关的信息。但表达的内容主要靠大脑记忆，而不是笔记。因此，表达时偶尔看一眼笔记上的相关数字、专有名词等即可，不能一味盯着笔记说译语。

3）看着笔记却说不出来，原因可能是：

- ✓ 笔记记得太多。

  改进办法：少记，用关键词、符号或缩略词等代表一串意思。

- ✓ 笔记符号不熟练，不知道该用什么符号怎么记，或者忘记了符号代表的意思。

  改进办法：跟同学对比笔记，互相借鉴。但不要背笔记符号，且在一个符号用稳定后再引入一个新的符号。

4）口译表达中的通病包括：

- ✓ 对词义的理解脱离上下文和语境。
- ✓ 笔记中记下的中文往往是字面意思。
- ✓ 译语啰唆、不准确。
- ✓ 把思考过程也说出来。
- ✓ 有复述或背课文的感觉（译给自己听），而不是给别人做口译的感觉（译给别人听）。
- ✓ ……

二、训练方法

- 总结训练中个人笔记的特点和问题：笔记多还是少？笔记的可利用程度如何？你个人认为采用何种方式记笔记能表达得更好？
- 小组口译练习。请没听过源语的同学听译语，指出译语中不清楚的地方。体会借助笔记的信息表达。
- 四人小组口译练习。两位同学记笔记并口译，一位同学评价译语准确性和完整性，另一位同学评价译员的眼神交流或肢体语言。依次互换角色，讨论和交流。

三、练习案例点评

──────────── 案例1 ────────────

源　　语： My dad's not alone. There's about 35 million people globally living with some kind of dementia, and by 2030 they're expecting that to double to 70 million. That's a lot of people. Dementia scares us. The confused faces and shaky hands of people who have dementia, the big numbers of people who get it … they frighten us. And because of that fear, we tend to do one of two things. We go into denial: "It's not me; it has nothing to do with me; it's never going to happen to me." Or, we decide that we're going to prevent dementia, and it will never happen to us because we're going to do everything right and it won't come and get us. I'm looking for a third way: I'm preparing to get Alzheimer's disease.

学生译语： 其实不止我父亲，这个世界上有三千五百万不同程度的阿兹海默症患者，而根据预测，到2030年这个数字还将翻一番，也就是七千九百万。阿兹海默症让人感到恐惧，人们会变得神志不清、双手颤抖，并且大量的患病人数都让人感到害怕。于是有些人就会开始否定这一切，他会觉得不是我得病，这件事……这个病和我一点关系都没有，永远也不会发生在我身上。还有些人会采取积极的预防措施，他们会做一切他们可以预防的方式，来保证阿兹海默症不会找上门来，也不会困扰我们。而我正在做的是第三种方式，就是为得这种病而做好准备。

> **点评**
>
> 1）大意比较完整，但需要提高译语表达。
>
> 2）第一句、第二句中，"而""并且"属于逻辑连接词冗余。
>
> 3）数字70 million没有译准确。And because of that fear, we tend to do one of two things 的后半句漏译。
>
> 4）"大量的患病人数"这样的表达显得奇怪，应改为"患病人数多"。
>
> 5）"他们会做一切他们可以预防的方式，来保证阿兹海默症（阿尔茨海默病）不会找上门来，也不会困扰我们"一句人称代词指代不明，应该统一。"做一切他们可以预防的方式"搭配不当。
>
> 6）"而我正在……就是为得这种病而做好准备"含义有偏差，似乎表示"我很希望得阿尔茨海默病"一样，可以适当增译为"为万一患病做准备"。
>
> 教师评分：89。

案例2

源　　语：Today we are launching a campaign called HeForShe. I am reaching out to you because we need your help. We want to end gender inequality, and to do this, we need everyone involved. This is the first campaign of its kind at the UN. We want to try and galvanize as many men and boys as possible to be advocates for change. And we don't just want to talk about it. We want to try and make sure that it's tangible.

学生译语：今天我们将要发起一个叫做HeForShe的活动。我站在这里是因为我需要你们的帮助，我们想要结束性别不平等，我们希望……而要做到这一点，我们需要每个人都参与其中。HeForShe是联合国第一次发起这一类活动。我们使尽可能多的男性和男孩也成为这次活动的倡导者。我们不仅仅是说说而已，我们也在努力尝试去让这个改变，变成有形的东西。

📋 点评

1）整体信息比较完整，但译语稍显啰嗦。有些译法拘泥于源语字面意思，如"成为这次活动的倡导者"。理解源语意思之后，再用译语说出同样的意思更有助于产出符合中文表达习惯的译语。

2）这篇材料的一个关键词就是HeForShe这个活动。学生可能因为不知道这个活动名称是否有固定的中文译法，又考虑到直译为"他为她"恐怕不易理解，所以直接重复源语HeForShe，并一直沿用下去。作为一种应对方法，这样也是可以的。

3）译语中的"我们"太多，造成冗余。大部分"我们"等人称代词在中文语境中可以不言自明，说了反而不够精炼。

4）有些表达啰嗦或别扭，如and make sure that it's tangible译为"变成有形的东西"有点太拘泥于字面，可以译成"让它看得见、摸得着"；"男性和男孩"表达别扭，直接译为"男性"即可。

教师评分：90。

四、篇章练习

生词表

英文	中文
Mulantou Lighthouse	木栏头灯塔（航标灯塔，位于海南省文昌市）
monetary tightening	货币紧缩

（待续）

（续表）

英文	中文
hub	枢纽，中心
depreciate	（货币）贬值，跌价
debt distress	债务困境
Common Framework	"共同框架"（二十国集团制定了"共同框架"，帮助最贫穷国家重组债务并解决偿付力丧失和长期存在的流动性问题）
Global Sovereign Debt Roundtable	全球主权债务圆桌会议
dementia	痴呆症
op-eds, opposite editorial	社论对页版（由报社外部人士撰写）
origami	折纸艺术
tremor	颤抖
Goodwill Ambassador for UN Women	联合国妇女署亲善大使
inadvertent	无意的

1）Navigate this time of global economic uncertainty

练习说明：

1. This is a speech made by Kristalina Georgieva, Managing Director of IMF, at the 2023 Boao Forum for Asia on March 30, 2023, where she talked about how policymakers navigate this time of global economic uncertainty. Before interpreting, be prepared for anything you think might be difficult to interpret, such as names of people, place, or institutions.

2. The speech is divided into nine segments. Record your interpretation at each stop signal.

3. After interpreting,

   1) review your recording for quality: Did you get the correct message? Does your retelling contain any language fillers, pauses longer than three seconds, disorganized information, or unidiomatic expressions?

   2) reflect upon your notes when listening to your interpretation. Were your notes helpful? Which one did you use more, your notes or your STM? How did you balance the two? Did you manage to only glance at your notes occasionally when interpreting? If not, interpret again until you acquire this note-reading skill.

   3) ask your peers to assess your interpretation without listening to the original speech. Is your Chinese interpretation concise, precise, and idiomatic? Think about how to improve it.

Your Excellency Premier Li Qiang,

Excellencies,

Ladies and gentlemen,

早上好, good morning!

It is very fitting to be here today. The Boao Forum for Asia is hosted by the home of Mulantou Lighthouse, the tallest in China, a beacon of light guiding ships to (a) safe harbor, as we ought to guide our world economy to a safer future.

It has been in choppy waters for quite some time, experiencing shock upon shock upon shock. We expect 2023 to be another difficult year, with global growth falling below three percent as the effects of the war in Ukraine and monetary tightening continue to take hold. A rapid transition from a prolonged period of low interest rates to much higher rates — necessary to fight inflation — has inevitably caused turbulence in the banking sector in some advanced economies and made policy choices even harder. Asia is a source of dynamism. We project this year China and India to contribute 50 percent of global growth. But Asia also feels uncertainty in the world we are living today.

So, how can policymakers navigate this time of uncertainty? This year's Boao Forum gives us an answer: through cooperation and solidarity, the twin beacons of light we can rely on to guide us through the challenges that lie ahead. We know that cooperation has already transformed the global economy by deepening trade integration — which has boosted incomes and living standards across the world.

Over the past 40 years, the world economy has tripled in size. Emerging markets and developing economies are the biggest beneficiaries: They have quadrupled. Rich countries have also benefited. They doubled. And here in China, 800 million people have been lifted out of poverty, as the country has become even more integrated into world economy. This is an incredible achievement. Likewise, in countries across Asia, trade integration has been a key ingredient of strong GDP growth for many decades — including trade within the region, which today accounts for almost 50 percent of the total with China being a critical hub.

But we must also recognize that the benefits of globalization have not been shared equally across countries or people. And we have learned that supply chains must be made more secure and more resilient. Addressing these concerns, as we heard from Premier Li Qiang — it requires a pragmatic approach — working together where it matters most, for example, to reinvigorate international trade in an equitable way and diversify supply chains based on economic logic. Our research shows that the long-term cost of trade fragmentation could be as high as seven percent of global GDP — roughly equivalent to the combined annual output of Germany and Japan. And as a highly integrated region, Asia would be most adversely affected by runaway fragmentation. We must keep this cost down through cooperation. It would be paramount for the prosperity of hundreds of millions of people around the world.

Cooperation goes hand in hand with solidarity with those in greatest need. Over the past three years, we have seen low-income and vulnerable countries and people being particularly severely hit. Solidarity starts at home, with governments protecting vulnerable people in their own countries. This means fiscal policy providing targeted support to those most in need, those most affected by food insecurity or the cost-of-living crisis.

And it also means countries in a relatively stronger position helping vulnerable members of our global community. With interest rates high and many currencies depreciating, this is particularly important for countries in debt distress. We urgently need faster and more efficient global mechanisms for providing debt treatment to these countries.

After all, such mechanisms would provide significant benefits to both creditors and debtors. And success would remove one important source of uncertainty for the global picture. And in this regard, I want to recognize with gratitude to China's engagement in the Common Framework for that resolution and China's participation in the new Global Sovereign Debt Roundtable. Solidarity must extend to future generations — and nowhere it matters more than in climate action, especially in Asia with its high population density and exposure to climate shocks. And it is also the place to steer, through the green transition, much needed opportunities for growth and for jobs.

Let me conclude by stating the obvious: Despite all the forces of fragmentation, we know — we know we are stronger together. Together, we can spread a guiding light far and wide. Together, we can navigate the rough waters to reach a safe harbor. Together, we are wealthier and more secure. 谢谢 [Thank you]!

----

2) How I'm preparing to get Alzheimer's disease

练习说明：
1. This is a talk in which the speaker shares what she had learned about Alzheimer's disease from taking care of her father. Brainstorm before listening: Do you have knowledge about Alzheimer's disease such as its symptoms, pathology, and caring?
2. The talk is divided into seven segments. Interpret the message at each stop signal and record your interpretation.

3. After interpreting,
   1) review your recording for quality: Did you get the correct message? Does your interpretation contain any language fillers, pauses longer than three seconds, disorganized information, or unidiomatic expressions?
   2) reflect upon your notes when listening to your interpretation. Which was more helpful when you delivered the message, your notes or your STM?
   3) think about the following questions: How did you interpret the informal and colloquial English expressions into idiomatic Chinese? Did you take notes more in English or in Chinese? What signs or symbols did you use and were they effective?

I'd like to talk about my dad. My dad has Alzheimer's disease. He started showing the symptoms about 12 years ago, and he was officially diagnosed in 2005. Now he's really pretty sick. He needs help eating; he needs help getting dressed; he doesn't really know where he is or when it is; and it's been really, really hard. My dad was my hero and my mentor for most of my life, and I've spent the last decade watching him disappear.

My dad's not alone. There's about 35 million people globally living with some kind of dementia, and by 2030 they're expecting that to double to 70 million. That's a lot of people. Dementia scares us. The confused faces and shaky hands of people who have dementia, the big numbers of people who get it … they frighten us. And because of that fear, we tend to do one of two things. We go into denial: "It's not me; it has nothing to do with me; it's never going to happen to me." Or, we decide that we're going to prevent dementia, and it will never happen to us because we're going to do everything right and it won't come and get us. I'm looking for a third way: I'm preparing to get Alzheimer's disease.

Prevention is good, and I'm doing the things that you can do to prevent Alzheimer's. I'm eating right; I'm exercising every day; I'm keeping my mind active. That's what the research says you should do. But the research also shows that there's nothing that will 100 percent protect you. If the monster wants you, the monster's gonna get you. That's what happened with my dad. My dad was a bilingual college professor. His hobbies were chess, bridge, and writing op-eds. He got dementia anyway. If the monster wants you, the monster's gonna get you. Especially if you're me, because Alzheimer's tends to run in families. So I'm preparing to get Alzheimer's disease.

Based on what I've learned from taking care of my father, and researching what it's like to live with dementia, I'm focusing on three things in my preparation: I'm changing what I do for fun; I'm working to build my physical strength; and — this is the hard one — I'm trying to become a better person.

Let's start with the hobbies. When you get dementia, it gets harder and harder to enjoy yourself. You can't sit and have long talks with your old friends, because you don't know who they are. It's confusing to watch television, and often very frightening. And reading is just about impossible. When you care for someone with dementia, and you get training, they train you to engage them in activities that are familiar, hands-on, open-ended. With my dad, that turned out to be letting him fill out forms. He was a college professor at a state school; he knows what paperwork looks like. He'll sign his name on every line; he'll check all the boxes; he'll put numbers in where he thinks there should be numbers.

But it got me thinking: What would my caregivers do with me? I'm my father's daughter. I read, I write, I think about global health a lot. Would they give me academic journals so I could scribble in the margins? Would they give me charts and graphs that I could color? So I've been trying to learn to do things that are hands-on. I've always liked to draw, so I'm doing it more even though I'm really very bad at it. I am learning some basic origami. I can make a really great box. And I'm teaching myself to knit, which … so far I can knit a blob.

But, you know, it doesn't matter if I'm actually good at it. What matters is that my hands know how to do it. Because the more things that are familiar, the more things my hands know how to do, the more things that I can be happy and busy doing when my brain's not running the show anymore. They say that people who are engaged in activities are happier, easier for their caregivers to look after, and it may even slow the progress of the disease. That all seems like win to me. I want to be as happy as I can for as long as I can.

A lot of people don't know that Alzheimer's actually has physical symptoms, as well as cognitive symptoms. You lose your sense of balance; you get muscle tremors, and that tends to lead people to being less and less mobile. They get scared to walk around. They get scared to move. So I'm doing activities that will build my sense of balance. I'm doing yoga and tai chi to improve my balance, so that when I start to lose it, I'll still be able to be mobile. I'm doing weight-bearing exercise, so that I have the muscle strength so that when I start to wither, I have more time (so) that I can still move around.

Finally, the third thing. I'm trying to become a better person. My dad was kind and loving before he had Alzheimer's, and he's kind and loving now. I've seen him lose his intellect, his sense of humor, his language skills, but I've also seen this: He loves me; he loves my sons; he loves my brother and my mom and his caregivers. And that love makes us want to be around him, even now, even when it's so hard. When you take away everything that he ever learned in this world, his naked heart still shines. I was never as kind as my dad, and I was never as loving. And what I need now is to learn to be like that. I need a heart so pure that if it's stripped bare by dementia, it will survive.

I don't want to get Alzheimer's disease. What I want is a cure in the next 20 years, soon enough to protect me. But if it comes for me, I'm going to be ready. Thank you.

3）HeForShe

练习说明：

1. This is a speech about gender inequality and how to fight it given by Emma Watson, a British actor and Goodwill Ambassador for UN Women. Think about the following questions: What strategies can be used to interpret such a polished and moving speech into Chinese? And how can notes be used effectively to achieve that goal?
2. The speech is divided into 10 segments. Interpret the message and record your interpretation at each stop signal.
3. After interpreting,
   1) review your recording for quality: Did you get the correct message? Does your interpretation contain any language fillers, pauses longer than three seconds, disorganized information, or unidiomatic expressions?
   2) listen to your interpretation ONLY. Does your Chinese interpretation sound clear and fluent? Does it make sense to the audience? Are there any ways to improve it? Did you find your notes helpful?

Your Excellencies,
UN Secretary-General,
President of the General Assembly,
Executive director of UN Women,
And distinguished Guests,

Today we are launching a campaign called HeForShe. I am reaching out to you because we need your help. We want to end gender inequality, and to do this, we need everyone involved. This is the first campaign of its kind at the UN. We want to try and galvanize as many men and boys as possible to be advocates for change. And we don't just want to talk about it. We want to try and make sure that it's tangible.

I was appointed as Goodwill Ambassador for UN Women six months ago. And, the more I spoke about feminism, the more I have realized that fighting for women's rights has too often become synonymous with man-hating. If there is one thing I know for certain, it is that this has to stop.

For the record, feminism by definition is the belief that men and women should have equal rights and opportunities. It is the theory of the political, economic, and social equality of the sexes.

I started questioning gender-based assumptions a long time ago. When I was eight, I was confused for being called "bossy" because I wanted to direct the plays that we would put on for our parents, but the boys were not. When at 14, I started to be sexualized by certain elements of the media. When at 15, my girlfriends started dropping out of their beloved sports teams because they didn't want to appear muscly. When at 18, my male friends were unable to express their feelings.

I decided that I was a feminist, and this seemed uncomplicated to me. But my recent research has shown me that "feminism" has become an unpopular word. Women are choosing not to identify as feminists. Apparently, I'm among the ranks of women whose expressions are seen as too strong, too aggressive, isolating, and anti-men. Unattractive, even.

Why has the word become such an uncomfortable one?

I am from Britain, and I think it is right I am paid the same as my male counterparts. I think it is right that I should be able to make decisions about my own body. I think it is right that women be involved on my behalf in the policies and decisions that will affect my life. I think it is right that socially, I am afforded the same respect as men.

But sadly, I can say that there is no one country in the world where all women can expect to receive these rights. No country in the world can yet say that they have achieved gender equality. These rights — I consider to be human rights. But I am one of the lucky ones.

My life is a sheer privilege because my parents didn't love me less because I was born a daughter. My school did not limit me because I was a girl. My mentors didn't assume that I would go less far because I might give birth to a child one day. These influencers were the gender equality ambassadors that made me who I am today. They may not know it, but they are the inadvertent feminists who are changing the world today. And we need more of those.

And if you still hate the word, it is not the word that is important. It's the idea and the ambition behind it, because not all women have received the same rights that I have. In fact, statistically, very few have ~~been~~.

Men, I would like to take this opportunity to extend your formal invitation. Gender equality is your issue, too.

Because to date, I've seen my father's role as a parent being valued less by society, despite my need of his presence as a child, as much as my mother's. I've seen young men suffering from mental illness, unable to ask for help for fear it would make them less of a man. In fact, in the U.K., suicide is the biggest killer of men between 20 to 49, eclipsing road accidents, cancer, and coronary heart disease. I've seen men made fragile and insecure by a distorted sense of what constitutes male success. Men don't have the benefits of equality, either.

We don't often talk about men being imprisoned by gender stereotypes, but I can see that they are, and that when they are free, things will change for women as a natural consequence. If men don't have to be aggressive in order to be accepted, women won't feel compelled to be submissive. If men don't have to control, women won't have to be controlled. Both men and women should feel free to be sensitive. Both men and women should feel free to be strong. It is time that we all perceived gender on a spectrum, instead of two sets of opposing ideals. If we stop defining each other by what we are not, and start defining ourselves by who we are, we can all be freer, and this is what HeForShe is about. It's about freedom.

I want men to take up this mantle so that their daughters, sisters, and mothers can be free from prejudice, but also so that their sons have permission to be vulnerable and human too, reclaim those parts of themselves they abandoned, and in doing so, be a more true and complete version of themselves.

You might be thinking, "Who is this Harry Potter girl, and what is she doing speaking at the UN?" And, it's a really good question. I've been asking myself the same thing.

All I know is that I care about this problem, and I want to make it better.

And, having seen what I've seen, and given the chance, I feel it is my responsibility to say something. Statesman Edmund Burke said, "All that is needed for the forces of evil to triumph is for the good men and women to do nothing."

In my nervousness for this speech and in my moments of doubt, I told myself firmly, "If not me, who? If not now, when?" If you have similar doubts when opportunities are presented to you, I hope that those words will be helpful. Because the reality is that if we do nothing, it will take 75 years, or for me to be nearly 100 before women can expect to be paid the same as men for the same work; 15.5 million girls will be married in the next 16 years as children. And at current rates, it won't be until 2086 before all rural African girls can have a secondary education.

If you believe in equality, you might be one of those inadvertent feminists that I spoke of earlier, and for this, I applaud you. We are struggling for a uniting word, but the good news is that we have a uniting movement. It is called HeForShe. I am inviting you to step forward, to be seen and to ask yourself, "If not me, who? If not now, when?"

Thank you very, very much.

五、补充阅读

1）雷天放，陈菁. 口译教程 [M]. 上海：上海外语教育出版社，2006.

2）苏伟，邓轶. 口译基础 [M]. 上海：上海外语教育出版社，2009.

3）仲伟合，王斌华. 基础口译 [M]. 北京：外语教学与研究出版社，2009.

测试和总结

一、测试说明

1）测试形式：

- 纯数字口译
- 带单位数字口译
- 口译含数字的句子
- 口译含数字的段落

2）交传的十一条原则：

① Memory is the key. Concentrate on listening and comprehension; note-taking is just a supporting tool to trigger your memory.

② Organize contents into concepts-pictures that are stored in your brain.

③ Start taking notes only after you understand completely what is said.

④ Mark the connection between sentences with small words, acronyms, letters, symbols, arrows, underlines, ticks, etc.

⑤ Stop taking notes when you're lost. Concentrate on listening, take down key words or phrases, and then go on.

⑥ Do not attempt to write down every word; the more notes you take, the more you forget.

⑦ Do not worry about losing things. When you find it difficult to catch up with the speaker, just listen carefully and take notes later, even though you've missed just two or three words.

⑧ Themes and logical flow are the most important elements to pay attention to. It's normal to drop some adjectives or adverbs, which, sometimes, are less important.

⑨ Keep your eyes on the speaker once in a while when taking notes. This will allow you to concentrate on listening and read the speaker's body languages, which are extremely important for you to remember what is said.

⑩ Never take down trivial words like *of*, *and*, 的, 了, 吗, etc. Consecutive note-taking is not speed writing. Again, the more you take down, the more you forget.

⑪ Use verticalization and indentation when taking notes. Draw a line between two meaning groups and a double line between paragraphs.

3）测试后填写"评估与反思"部分的自评互评表和总结。

二、测试题

This test is divided into FOUR groups.

Group 1 consists of 10 bare numbers, while **Group 2** consists of 10 numbers with units. The 10 numbers in each group will be provided consecutively without any interruptions. Please take notes and interpret them into Chinese after the signal.

Group 3 consists of four sentences with numbers. Please take notes and interpret each sentence into Chinese after the signal.

Group 4 consists of two paragraphs, each of which is made up of four sentences. One is about the 2022 Winter Olympics, and the other one is about U.S. trade. Please take notes and interpret each paragraph into Chinese after the signal.

三、评估与反思

笔记测试自评互评表

被评人：   评分人：

总分：

填表日期：

填表说明：
1. 某项（如错误、原因、办法等）罗列的行数可根据其数量相应增加或减少。
2. 不必把源语转录成文字。
3. 根据表格中的标注填写自评和互评。

第一组：纯数字

数字反应准确且快（10*1分=10分），互评人填写

		被评人译本	正确的译本
译错的地方	1.		
	2.		
	3.		
错误原因	1.		
	2.		
	3.		

（待续）

解决办法	1.	
	2.	
	3.	
被评人得分		

第二组：带单位数字

数字（1分）和单位（1分）无错、漏（10*2分=20分），互评人填写

	被评人译本	正确的译本
译错的地方	1.	
	2.	
	3.	
错误原因	数字	
	单位	
解决办法	1.	
	2.	
	3.	
被评人得分		

第三组：含数字的句子

信息（2分）、数字（2分）、单位（1分）齐全（4*5分=20分），互评人填写

被评人译本 （请将译语录音 转为文字）	1.	
	2.	
	3.	
	4.	
译错的地方	信息	
	数字	
	单位	
错误原因	1.	
	2.	
	3.	
解决办法	1.	
	2.	
	3.	
被评人得分		

第四组：含数字的段落

句子逻辑和框架（10分）、数字和单位（10分）、表达（5分）正确（2*25分=50分），互评人填写

第一段	被评人说的大意是什么？	是否抓准了大意？	
	被评人译本录音转写：	有无可以改进的地方？	
第二段	被评人说的大意是什么？	是否抓准了大意？	
	被评人译本录音转写：	有无可以改进的地方？	
译错的地方	逻辑和框架		
	数字和单位		
	表达		
错误原因	1.		
	2.		
	3.		
解决办法	1.		
	2.		
	3.		
被评人得分	第一段：		第二段：

对本次测试的自我总结和反思，被评人填写

对笔记训练阶段的总结和整体感受，被评人填写

综合训练

第**11**章 ▶ 跨文化意识

一、技能解说

1）意识（awareness）是了解或知道；能力（competence）是运用。能力培养先从培养意识开始，经过较长时间的刻意练习，意识可能逐渐转变为能力。

2）口译中的跨文化意识是指对本文化有充分了解的同时，具备其他文化的相关知识，熟知如何与具有其他文化背景的人沟通、互动和共事。跨文化能力是指对源语和目的语之间、发言者和听众之间的文化差异具备敏感性和判断力，成功协助双方实现信息、观点和思想的交流。

3）培养跨文化意识可以从扩大知识面和视野开始。对待不同文化差异，应一视同仁，以听众为本；吸取经验，多总结（雷天放、陈菁，2006，p. 188）。

4）英语文化中的文化禁忌（taboos）、盲点（blind spots）、潜在含义（implied meaning）、双关（puns）、笑话（jokes）、轶事（anecdotes）、俚语（slangs）、幽默（humor）等都可能造成沟通障碍，此时译员应发挥"协调人"（mediator）作用，采取意译（free translation）、转换（conversion）、阐释（paraphrasing）、增补（addition）或省略（omission）等方法，帮助实现跨文化沟通。

二、训练方法

- 收集和学习英文笑话、俗语、俚语、名言警句等，在小组练习中提供给同伴练习并解释。
- 一句多译练习。小组成员说一句长英文，其余组员轮流用不同的主语开头进行口译，然后交换角色。体会一旦"胸有成竹"（源语意义已经掌握），就能"出口成章"（无论用何开头都能说下去并译全）的感觉。
- 给自己的口译录音，请没听过源语的同伴听译语，逐句指出所有中文表达有些奇怪的地方。反复体会和琢磨如何实现简洁和地道的中文表达。

三、练习案例点评

—————————————————— 案例1 ——————————————————

源　语：Thank you. I am honored to be with you today for your commencement from one of the finest universities in the world. Truth be told, I never graduated from college, and this is the closest I've ever gotten to a college graduation. Today I want to tell you three stories from my life. That's it. No big deal. Just three stories.

The first story is about connecting the dots. I dropped out of Reed College after the first six months, but then stayed around as a drop-in for another 18 months or so before I really quit. So why did I drop out?

It started before I was born. My biological mother was a young, unwed graduate student, and she decided to put me up for adoption. She felt very strongly that I should be adopted by college graduates, so everything was all set for me to be adopted at birth by a lawyer and his wife.

学生译语： 谢谢大家，我很荣幸参加大家的毕业典礼，嗯，在这所世界名校。说实话，我大学没有毕业，这是我距离大学毕业典礼最近的一次。嗯，今天我想和大家分享三个我人生中的故事，没什么大不了，就三个故事而已。第一个故事是……是我大学辍学的故事。我辍学后又当了18个月的……嗯……drop-in才真正离开大学。我为什么要辍学？这要从我出生那天说起。我的生母是个年轻的未婚大学生，她决定把我送给别人收养。她认为我一定要被大学生，要被念过大学的人领养。所以我将会被一个律师和他的妻子收养。

点评

1）整体译文的逻辑和信息是完整的。

2）但是很多表达很别扭，不符合汉语的表达习惯。译语拘泥于源语用词或句式，比如"我很荣幸参加大家的毕业典礼，嗯，在这所世界名校""她认为我一定要被大学生，要被念过大学的人领养"。可能的原因是笔记记的是英文的用词和结构，没有把理解后的意思记下来；或者看笔记回忆的时候没有边想边监听输出、修改遣词造句，没有按中文习惯重新组织句子表达。学生记笔记的时候，总想把所有信息都记下来，会出现"顾此失彼"的情况。鼓励多用中文记理解后的内容，并少记笔记。

3）出现三次"嗯"这类的填充词，一次三秒以上的停顿，一次重复，一次自我修正。应该养成习惯，尽量避免这些问题。

4）没听懂connecting the dots、Reed College、drop-in等词语，导致漏译。比如，connecting the dots是西方儿童"连点成形"的小游戏，没译出来可能是因为不了解。演讲开头提出的概念常常会在演讲中途详细阐述，一开始就要译准确的确不容易。因此，应该做充足的译前准备，平时多积累和了解英语国家的文化。

译前准备，平时多积累和了解英语国家的文化。

教师评分：85。

源　　语：So my parents, who were on a waiting list, got a call in the middle of the night asking, "We've got an unexpected baby boy. Do you want him?" They said, "Of course." My biological mother found out later that my mother had never graduated from college and that my father had never graduated from high school. She refused to sign the final adoption papers. She only relented a few months later when my parents promised that I would go to college. This was the start in [of] my life.

学生译语：所以，我真正的养父母在一天深夜接到了一个电话，电话里说："现在我们有一个男婴，你们想要吗？"他们回答说："当然想。"但是我的亲生母亲却发现我的养母没有上过大学，而养父甚至连高中都没毕业，所以，她拒绝签这份收养协议。直到几个月后，我的养父母承诺会让我上大学后，我生母的态度才有所改观。这是我人生的开端。

📋 点评

1）译语总体不错，但部分表达带有翻译腔。

2）"真正的养父母"翻译得很拗口，可以直接译为"养父母"。养父母的回答"当然想"改译成"当然要"会更自然。在翻译直接引语如问答时，常常要避免逐字译。

3）拘泥于源语用词或句式容易导致译语翻译腔。理解了源语意思后，应该"扔掉"源语的句法、语法，用地道的译语语言表达出来，或根据语境调整译文，使之符合一定的情感基调。比如在译最后一句的时候，需要结合之前提到的生母、养母甚至差点被弃养等细节，如果译为"这是我人生的开端"就显得不到位。

教师评分：89。

四、篇章练习

生词表

英文	中文
nom de plume	笔名
general dentistry	牙科
perspire	出汗
steroid	类固醇

（待续）

英文	中文
intercontinental	洲际的
cranium	颅腔
thorax	胸腔
abdominal cavity	腹腔
fibula	腓骨
varicose	静脉曲张
Caesarean section	剖宫产
Fat Tuesday, Mardi Gras	油腻星期二（新奥尔良狂欢节，人们会播撒三色珠串庆祝节日）
tequila	龙舌兰酒
connecting the dots	连点成形（一种儿童游戏）
drop-in	旁听生
serif	衬线（字体）
san serif	无衬线（字体）
karma	因果报应，因缘
baton	指挥棒，接力棒
Pixar	皮克斯动画工作室
tumor	肿瘤
biopsy	活检，活体组织切片检查
endoscope	内窥镜
intestines	肠
sedate	给⋯服镇静剂
dogma	教条
Polaroid camera	拍立得照相机
paperback	平装书

1）Talks with jokes

练习说明：

1. The following are 14 jokes. Can you find their punch lines? How to interpret them properly into Chinese? Think of the possible challenges for interpreting.
2. Create some mini-talks with those jokes, and tell them to your peers. Ask your peers to interpret by turns in group practice. Do their interpretations sound like a joke? Why

or why not? Can you come up with more ways to interpret these jokes in your talks? Discuss with your peers.

A clergyman and a lion met. Clergyman prayed: "God, please save me!" So did the lion. The clergyman asked: "Why?" The lion answered: "Pray for my saving grace."

Rob and Tom apply for the same job. They take a written test. "You both got the same number of questions wrong," the HR person tells them, "but Rob gets the job." "If we both got the same number of questions wrong, how come he gets the job?" Tom asked indignantly. "Well," says the HR person, "one of his incorrect answers was better than yours." "Whoa, how can that be?" "For problem No. 46, Rob wrote, 'I don't know.' You wrote, 'Me neither.'"

Some writers use a nom de plume instead of their real names. I took my younger brother to a dentist who should try a nom de doctor. The nameplate outside his office read: "General Dentistry, Dr. Will Hurt."

Q: Name the four seasons.
A: Salt, pepper, mustard and vinegar.

Q: Explain one of the processes by which water can be made safe to drink.
A: Filter makes water safe to drink because it removes large pollutants like grit, sand, dead sheep and canoeists.

Q: How is dew formed?
A: The sun shines down on the leaves and makes them perspire.

Q: How can you delay milk turning sour?
A: Keep it in the cow.

Q: What causes the tides in the oceans?
A: The tides are a fight between the Earth and the Moon. All water tends to flow towards the Moon, because there is no water on the Moon, and nature hates a vacuum. I forget where the Sun joins in this fight.

Q: What are steroids?
A: Things for keeping carpets still on the stairs.

Q: What happens to your body as you age?

A: When you get old, so do your bowels and you get intercontinental.

Q: How are the main parts of the body categorized? (e.g., abdomen)

A: The body consists of three parts — the cranium, the thorax and the abdominal cavity. The cranium contains the brain; the thorax contains the heart and lungs, and the abdominal cavity contains the five bowels A, E, I, O, and U.

Q: What is the fibula?

A: A small lie.

Q: What does "varicose" mean?

A: Nearby.

Q: Give the meaning of the term "Caesarean section."

A: The Caesarean section is a district in Rome.

Q: What does the word "benign" mean?

A: Benign is what you will be after you "be eight."

2）Ellen DeGeneres's commencement address

练习说明：

1. This material includes the opening and concluding parts of Ellen's commencement address at Tulane in New Orleans given in 2009. Ellen hosts "Ellen DeGeneres's Show" on TV and is known for her humorous way of talking. Besides her witty remarks, her speech contains names, slangs, jokes, colloquial expressions, humor, satire, etc. How to properly interpret these elements? Think before you interpret.

2. Record your interpretation at each stop signal.

3. After interpreting,

   1) review your recording for quality: Does your interpretation contain any language fillers, pauses longer than three seconds, disorganized information, or unidiomatic expressions?

   2) reflect upon your notes and think about the following questions: Did you manage to glance at your notes only occasionally when interpreting? Did your notes fail you or help you interpret better? Why? For those seemingly uninterpretable jokes, how did you interpret them? Discuss with your peers.

Excerpt 1

Thank you, President Cowen, Mrs. President Cowen; distinguished guests, undistinguished guests — you know who you are; honored faculty, and creepy Spanish teachers.

And thank you to all the graduating class of 2009. I realize most of you are hungover and have splitting headaches and haven't slept since Fat Tuesday, but you can't graduate 'til I finish, so listen up.

When I was asked to make the commencement speech, I immediately said yes. Then I went to look up what commencement meant — which would have been easy if I had a dictionary, but most of the books in our house are Portia's, and they're all written in Australian.

So I had to break the word down myself, to find out the meaning. Commencement: common, and cement. Common cement. You commonly see cement on sidewalks. Sidewalks have cracks, and if you step on a crack, you break your mother's back. So there's that.

But I'm honored that you've asked me here to speak at your "common cement."

I thought that you had to be a famous alumnus – alumini – aluminum – alumis — you had to graduate from this school. And I didn't go to college here … and I don't know if President Cowen knows, I didn't go to any college at all. Any college. And I'm not saying you wasted your time, or money, but look at me, I'm a huge celebrity.

Although I did graduate from the school of hard knocks, our mascot was the knockers.

I spent a lot of time here growing up. My mom worked at Newcomb and I would go there every time I needed to steal something out of her purse.

But why am I here today? Clearly not to steal, you're too far away and I'd never get away with it. I'm here because of you. Because I can't think of a more tenacious, more courageous graduating class. I mean, look at you all, wearing your robes. Usually when you're wearing a robe at 10 in the morning, it means you've given up.

Excerpt 2

But my idea of success is different today and as you grow, you'll realize definition of success changes. For me, the most important thing in your life is to live your life with integrity, and not to give in to peer pressure; to try to be something that you're not; to live your life as an honest and compassionate person; to contribute in some way.

So to conclude my conclusion: Follow your passion, stay true to yourself. Never follow someone else's path, unless you're in the woods and you're lost and you see a path, and by all means you should follow that.

Don't give advice; it will come back and bite you in the ass. Don't take anyone's advice. So my advice to you is to be true to yourself and everything will be fine. And I know that a lot of you are concerned about your future, but there's no need to worry. The economy is booming, the job market is wide open, the planet is just fine. It's going to be great.

You've already survived a hurricane. What else can happen to you? And as I mentioned before, some of the most devastating things that happen to you will teach you the most. And now you know the right questions to ask for your first job interview, like "Is it above sea level?"

So to conclude my conclusion that I've previously concluded, in the "common cement" speech, I guess what I'm trying to say is life is like one big Mardi Gras. But instead, show people your brain, and if they like what they see, you'll have more beads than you know what to do with.

So the Katrina class of 2009, I say congratulations and if you don't remember a thing I said today, remember this: You're gonna be OK, dum de dum dum dum, just dance.

3）Stay hungry, stay foolish

练习说明：

1. This is Steve Jobs' commencement address at Stanford University. In this speech, he shared three stories in his life. Brainstorm before listening: What do you know about Steve Jobs? What do you expect his life stories to be like? What are the characteristics of a commencement speech in terms of the language, format, etc.? What might be difficult to interpret?

2. The speech is divided into 10 segments. Record your interpretation at each stop signal.

3. After interpreting,

    1) review your recording for quality: Does your interpretation contain any language fillers, pauses longer than three seconds, disorganized information or unidiomatic expressions?

    2) when listening to your own recordings, check for mis-interpretations, self-repairs or false start, inappropriate pauses, etc., and consider what had caused these problems. Did your notes work? How can you improve them?

    3) think of the following questions: How did your Chinese interpretation sound? Was

it too formal/informal, or too literal/colloquial? How did you interpret those simple yet meaningful expressions, like "connecting the dots," "it would all work out OK," "not changed that one bit," "but I was still in love," "it was awful tasting medicine," "as with all matters of the heart," "you are already naked," "there is no reason not to follow your heart," etc.?

Thank you. I am honored to be with you today for your commencement from one of the finest universities in the world. Truth be told, I never graduated from college, and this is the closest I've ever gotten to a college graduation. Today I want to tell you three stories from my life. That's it. No big deal. Just three stories.

The first story is about connecting the dots. I dropped out of Reed College after the first six months, but then stayed around as a drop-in for another 18 months or so before I really quit. So why did I drop out?

It started before I was born. My biological mother was a young, unwed graduate student, and she decided to put me up for adoption. She felt very strongly that I should be adopted by college graduates, so everything was all set for me to be adopted at birth by a lawyer and his wife. Except that when I popped out, they decided at the last minute that they really wanted a girl.

So my parents, who were on a waiting list, got a call in the middle of the night asking, "We've got an unexpected baby boy. Do you want him?" They said, "Of course." My biological mother found out later that my mother had never graduated from college and that my father had never graduated from high school. She refused to sign the final adoption papers. She only relented a few months later when my parents promised that I would go to college. This was the start ~~in~~ [of] my life.

And 17 years later, I did go to college. But I naively chose a college that was almost as expensive as Stanford, and all of my working-class parents' savings were being spent on my college tuition. After six months, I couldn't see the value in it. I had no idea what I wanted to do with my life and no idea how college was going to help me figure it out. And here I was spending all of the money my parents had saved their entire life. So I decided to drop out and trust that it would all work out OK. It was pretty scary at the time, but looking back it was one of the best decisions I've ever made. The minute I dropped out I could stop taking the required classes that didn't interest me, and begin dropping in on the ones that looked far more interesting.

It wasn't all romantic. I didn't have a dorm room, so I slept on the floor in friends' rooms, I returned coke bottles for the five cents deposits to buy food with, and I would walk the seven miles across town every Sunday night to get one good meal a week at the Hare Krishna temple. I loved it. And much of what I stumbled into by following my curiosity and intuition turned out to be priceless later on.

Let me give you one example: Reed College at that time offered perhaps the best calligraphy instruction in the country. Throughout the campus every poster, every label on every drawer was beautifully hand calligraphed. Because I had dropped out and didn't have to take the normal classes, I decided to take a calligraphy class to learn how to do this. I learned about serif and san serif typefaces, about varying the amount of space between different letter combinations, about what makes great typography great. It was beautiful, historical, artistically subtle in a way that science can't capture, and I found it fascinating.

None of this had even a hope of any practical application in my life. But 10 years later, when we were designing the first Macintosh computer, it all came back to me. And we designed it all into the Mac. It was the first computer with beautiful typography. If I had never dropped in on that single course in college, the Mac would have never had multiple typefaces or proportionally spaced fonts. And since Windows just copied the Mac, it's likely that no personal computer would have them. If I had never dropped out, I would have never dropped in on that calligraphy class, and personal computers might not have the wonderful typography that they do. Of course it was impossible to connect the dots looking forward when I was in college. But it was very, very clear looking backwards 10 years later.

Again, you can't connect the dots looking forward. You can only connect them looking backwards. So you have to trust that the dots will somehow connect in your future. You have to trust in something — your gut, destiny, life, karma, whatever. Because believing that the dots would connect down the road will give you the confidence to follow your heart, even when it leads you off the well-known path, and that will make all the difference.

My second story is about love and loss.

I was lucky — I found what I loved to do early in life. Woz and I started Apple in my parents' garage when I was 20. We worked hard, and in 10 years Apple had grown from just the two of us in a garage into a two-billion-dollar company with over 4,000 employees. We had just released our finest creation — the Macintosh — a year earlier, and I (had) just turned 30. And then I got fired. How can you get fired from a company you started? Well, as Apple grew, we hired someone who I thought was very talented to run the company with me, and for the first year or so things went well. But then our visions of the future began to diverge and eventually we had a falling out. When we did, our Board of Directors sided with him. So at 30 I was out. And very publicly out. What had been the focus of my entire adult life was gone, and it was devastating.

I really didn't know what to do for a few months. I felt that I had let the previous generation of entrepreneurs down — that I had dropped the baton as it was being passed to me. I met with David Packard and Bob Noyce and tried to apologize for screwing up so badly. I was a very public failure, and I even thought about running away from the valley. But something slowly began to dawn on me — I still loved what I did. The turn of events at Apple had not changed that one bit. I had been rejected, but I was still in love. And so I decided to start over.

I didn't see it then, but it turned out that getting fired from Apple was the best thing that could have ever happened to me. The heaviness of being successful was replaced by the lightness of being a beginner again, less sure about everything. It freed me to enter one of the most creative periods of my life.

During the next five years, I started a company named NeXT, another company named Pixar, and fell in love with an amazing woman who would become my wife. Pixar went on to create the world's first computer-animated feature film, *Toy Story*, and is now the most successful animation studio in the world. In a remarkable turn of events, Apple bought NeXT, and I returned to Apple, and the technology we developed at NeXT is at the heart of Apple's current renaissance. And Laurene and I have a wonderful family together.

I'm pretty sure none of this would have happened if I hadn't been fired from Apple. It was awful tasting medicine, but I guess the patient needed it. Sometimes life is gonna hit you in the head with a brick. Don't lose faith. I'm convinced that the only thing that kept me going was that I loved what I did. You've got to find what you love. And that is as true for work as it is for your lovers. Your work is going to fill a large part of your life, and the only way to be truly satisfied is to do what you believe is great work. And the only way to do great work is to love what you do. If you haven't found it yet, keep looking, and don't settle. As with all matters of the heart, you'll know when you find it. And, like any great relationship, it just gets better and better as the years roll on. So keep looking. Don't settle.

My third story is about death.

When I was 17, I read a quote that went something like "If you live each day as if it was your last, someday you'll most certainly be right." It made an impression on me, and since then, for the past 33 years, I have looked in the mirror every morning and asked myself: "If today were the last day of my life, would I want to do what I am about to do today?" And whenever the answer has been "no" for too many days in a row, I know I need to change something.

Remembering that I'll be dead soon is the most important tool I've ever encountered to help me make the big choices in life. Because almost everything — all external expectations, all pride, all fear of embarrassment or failure — these things just fall away in the face of death, leaving only what is truly important. Remembering that you are going to die is the best way I know to avoid the trap of thinking you have something to lose. You are already naked. There is no reason not to follow your heart.

About a year ago I was diagnosed with cancer. I had a scan at 7:30 in the morning, and it clearly showed a tumor on my pancreas. I didn't even know what a pancreas was. The doctors told me this was almost certainly a type of cancer that is incurable, and that I should expect to live no longer than three to six months. My doctor advised me to go home and get my affairs in order, which is doctor's code for ~~prepare~~ [preparing] to die. It means to try and tell your kids everything you thought you'd have the next 10 years to tell them in just a few months. It means to make sure everything is buttoned up so that it will be as easy as possible for your family. It means to say your goodbyes.

I lived with that diagnosis all day. Later that evening I had a biopsy, where they stuck an endoscope down my throat, through my stomach and into my intestines, put a needle into my pancreas and got a few cells from the tumor. I was sedated, but my wife, who was there, told me that when they viewed the cells under a microscope the doctors started crying because it turned out to be a very rare form of pancreatic cancer that is curable with surgery. I had the surgery and thankfully, I'm fine now.

This was the closest I've been to facing death, and I hope it's the closest I get for a few more decades. Having lived through it, I can now say this to you with a bit more certainty than when death was a useful but purely intellectual concept:

No one wants to die. Even people who want to go to heaven don't want to die to get there. And yet death is the destination we all share. No one has ever escaped it. And that is as it should be, because Death is very likely the single best invention of Life. It is Life's change agent. It clears out the old to make way for the new. Right now the new is you, but someday not too long from now, you will gradually become the old and be cleared away. Sorry to be so dramatic, but it is quite true.

Your time is limited, so don't waste it living someone else's life. Don't be trapped by dogma — which is living with the results of other people's thinking. Don't let the noise of others' opinions drown out your own inner voice. And most important — have the courage to follow your heart and intuition. They somehow already know what you truly want to become. Everything else is secondary.

When I was young, there was an amazing publication called *The Whole Earth Catalog*, which was one of the bibles of my generation. It was created by a fellow named Stewart Brand not far from here in Menlo Park, and he brought it to life with his poetic touch. This was in the late sixties, before personal computers and desktop publishing, so it was all made with typewriters, scissors, and Polaroid cameras. It was sort of like Google in paperback form, 35 years before Google came along: It was idealistic, overflowing with neat tools and great notions.

Stewart and his team put out several issues of *The Whole Earth Catalog*, and then when it had run its course, they put out a final issue. It was the mid-1970s, and I was your age. On the back cover of their final issue was a photograph of an early morning country road, the kind you might find yourself hitchhiking on if you were so adventurous. Beneath it were the words: "Stay Hungry. Stay Foolish." It was their farewell message as they signed off. Stay hungry. Stay foolish. And I have always wished that for myself. And now, as you graduate to begin anew, I wish that for you.

Stay hungry. Stay foolish. Thank you all very much.

五、补充阅读

1）雷天放，陈菁. 口译教程 [M]. 上海：上海外语教育出版社，2006.

2）卢信朝. 英汉口译技能教程：口译 [M]. 北京：旅游教育出版社，2009.

3）仲伟合. 英语口译基础教程 [M]. 北京：高等教育出版社，2007.

第**12**章 ▶ 口译中的公共演说能力

一、技能解说

1）口译活动中，译员是仅次于讲话者的发言人，言行举止都受人关注。无论观众或听众数量多少，译员都应表现出一位优秀的发言者应有的样子。

2）人际沟通中，55%的信息通过面部表情（facial expression）和肢体语言（body language）传达，38%的信息通过声音呈现（vocal rendering）传递，只有7%是通过信息内容（content）本身。可见比起信息本身，信息如何传达更重要。

3）除语言外，副语言（paralanguage）和身势语（kinesics）都传递重要的口译信息（Poyatos，2001），其语用效果可分为伴随、替代、证明和否定。副语言包括停顿（pause）、填充词（filler）、语速（tempo）、音量（volume）、拖音（drawling）等声音特征（张威，2015）；身势语包括面部表情（facial expression）、眼神交流（eye-contact）、肢体语言（gesture）、仪态（manner）和体态（posture）等非声音特征。

二、训练方法

● 即兴演讲训练。
  1）小组练习，随机就某个话题发表3分钟即兴演讲，中英文皆可，并录像。
  2）回放录像，请同伴点评内容是否合理、有逻辑，以及面部表情、肢体语言、声音等是否得当。
  3）从讲话者的角度思考：如何做一个对译员友好的讲话者？
● 回放自己印象深刻的译员录像或录音，分析其副语言和身势语信息。列出其做得好的地方、指出可以改进的地方，并分析可能的原因。
● 小组练习口译并录像。对照同伴的录像评估自己的表现，或请同伴点评自己的口译录像。
● 小组讨论：不同口译场合中，译员应该怎么站、站哪里？译员应该怎么坐、坐哪里？译员的嘴离麦克风多远声音才合适？你会面对镜头口译吗？你口译时有小动作吗？译员应该如何着装？

三、练习案例点评

───────────── 案例1 ─────────────

源　　语： Dear fellow Olympians,

Your Olympic stage is set.

You have arrived here after overcoming so many challenges, living through great uncertainty. But now your moment has come: the moment you have been longing for — the moment we all have been longing for.

Now — your Olympic dream is coming true — in magnificent venues, supported by hundreds of millions of new Chinese winter sport fans.

学生译语： 亲爱的奥运会运动员们，奥运舞台已经就绪，你们克服了很多的困难挑战，经历了很多的动荡不安才来到这里，属于你们的时刻已经到来，你们所期盼的，也是我们所期盼的这一刻已经到来。你们的奥运梦想快要成真了，这里不仅场馆宏伟，还有几百万的中国冬季奥运会粉丝的支持。

📋 点评

1) 这段译语大意比较准确和完整，但是一些表达不够合适。"亲爱的奥运会运动员们"不如"各位奥林匹克运动员"的称呼正式。"奥运梦想快要成真"不如"梦想实现"表达恰当、地道。"这里不仅场馆宏伟，还有几百万的中国冬季奥运会粉丝的支持"比较口语化，不够正式。

2) 译语"还有几百万的中国冬季奥运会粉丝的支持"中，"几百万"属于数字理解错误，原文为hundreds of millions。

3) 最后一句漏译了new。这个词的含义很重要，"带动三亿人参与冰雪运动"是申办冬奥的一项重要目标。

4) 正式、官方的国际大型体育赛事的源语演讲，译语一定要有听众意识，要符合口译场合的需要，尤其是面对全球中文观众的实况转播演讲。多学习甚至适当背诵类似场合的译语会有帮助。

教师评分：75。

—— 案例2 ——

源　　语：Now … here's my brain. There is a difference. Both brains have a Rational Decision-Maker in them, but the procrastinator's brain also has an Instant Gratification Monkey. Now, what does this mean for the procrastinator? Well, it means everything's fine until this happens:

(a picture showing a dialog between two characters)
[This is a perfect time to get some work done.] [Nope!]

So the Rational Decision-Maker will make the rational decision to do something productive, but the Monkey doesn't like that Plan, so he actually takes the wheel, and he says, "Actually, let's read the entire Wikipedia page of the Nancy Kerrigan/Tonya Harding scandal, because I just remembered that that happened."

学生译语：这是我的大脑，两者大脑里都有一个理性决策者，但拖延症的大脑里有一只猴子，他需要即刻满足才行。这是什么意思？一切都好说，但这样不行。理性决策人说，咱们干点有意义的事情吧，但猴子不干，他掌控着方向盘说："我们来看看维基百科吧，看看这两个人的丑闻怎么样？我刚想起来。"

📖 点评

1）此段译语大意比较完整和准确，译法灵活。Instant Gratification Monkey译为"有一只猴子，他需要即刻满足才行"可以接受。Nancy Kerrigan/Tonya Harding scandal译为"这两个人的丑闻"应对恰当，虽没有译出人名，但意思是两人之间的丑闻，并不妨碍沟通。

2）译语"一切都好说，但这样不行"中"这样"的含义模糊，不便理解。

3）这个演讲语速较快，此段涉及一些口译难点，包括两个专有名词、一个人名/事件，以及until this happens中this指的是接下来的一段对话这个不易判断的点。如果译员能在记笔记的同时瞟一眼视频会有助于理解，且不容易混淆演讲本身和直接引用。

教师评分：85。

四、篇章练习

生词表

英文	中文
ambition	雄心
ski resort	滑雪场
ice rink	滑冰场
enthusiast	爱好者
gracious	亲切的，有礼貌的，和蔼的
Olympian	奥林匹克运动员
Olympic Truce Resolution	《奥林匹克休战决议》
bump up	增加，提高
(go) into high gear	（变得）非常活跃、兴奋或高效
pull an all-nighter	通宵学习
slow motion	电影中的特写慢镜头
gratification	满足，满意
epiphany	（对重要事物的）顿悟

1）Different interpreting styles

练习说明：

1. The following are six video or audio clips of interpreters at work. Identify their working mode (simultaneous, consecutive, liaison and sign language interpreting, etc.) and list as many as possible their paralanguage and kinesics information that you have noticed.

2. Do they look or sound like professional interpreters? Why or why not? Discuss with your peers.

Segment 1: T&I Professors from Monterrey demonstrate interpreting

----

Segment 2: Chinese-English onsite simultaneous interpretation

----

Segment 3: Interpreter protocol and standard of practice

Segment 4: How interpreters do their jobs

Segment 5: Deaf interpreters at work

Segment 6: Concert sign language interpreter

2）Speech for the opening ceremony of the Olympic Winter Games Beijing 2022

练习说明:

1. This is a ceremonial speech for the opening of 2022 Winter Olympics by International Olympic Committee (IOC) President Thomas Bach. Brainstorm before listening: What would possibly be the content of this speech?

2. The speech is simple, short but meaningful, and it was broadcast live to the world. Imagine you are interpreting for audiences all across China and abroad. How would you articulate the message and manage your voice? What would be the proper speed of interpreting?

3. The speech is divided into seven segments in this practice. Interpret the message at each stop signal and record your interpretation by making a video.

4. After interpreting,

   1) review your recording for quality: Do you look professional? Does your interpretation contain any language fillers, pauses longer than three seconds, disorganized information, or unidiomatic expressions? Compare yours with the live interpretation.

   2) assess your own performance in terms of language quality, paralanguage and kinesics.

…

Chers amis olympiques, [Dear Olympic friends,]
Welcome to the Olympic Winter Games Beijing 2022.
To all our Chinese friends: a very happy new year.
新春快乐，虎年大吉！[Happy New Year! Best wishes for the Year of the Tiger!]

This Year of the Tiger is also an Olympic Year. Both the Year of the Tiger and the Olympic Year stand for ambition, courage and strength.

Today, thanks to this ambition, China is a winter sport country. Well over 300 million people are engaged in winter sports in about 2,000 ski resorts and ice rinks. This extraordinary achievement opens a new era for global winter sport. It will raise the global participation to new levels, benefiting the Chinese people as well as winter sport enthusiasts around the world.

We can only write this new chapter in sporting history, because of our gracious hosts — the Chinese people, whom we thank wholeheartedly for welcoming us all so warmly. 谢谢你们，中国朋友！[Thank you, our Chinese friends!]

A special ~~thanks~~ [thank] goes to all the volunteers. You make us feel at home from the very first moment we arrived. Your smiling eyes are warming our hearts. Thank you volunteers.

Unfortunately, the global pandemic is still a reality for all of us. Therefore, our gratitude is even deeper for the Beijing 2022 Organizing Committee, the public authorities and all the Chinese people. Thank you for making these Olympic Winter Games happen — and making them happen in a safe way for everyone.

We all could only get here because of the countless medical workers, doctors, scientists, everybody in China and around the world who is going beyond the call of duty. Thank you for your outstanding efforts and solidarity.

In the same spirit, our heart goes out to all the athletes who, because of the pandemic, can not make their Olympic dream come true.

Dear fellow Olympians,

Your Olympic stage is set.

You have arrived here after overcoming so many challenges, living through great uncertainty. But now your moment has come: the moment you have been longing for — the moment we all have been longing for.

Now — your Olympic dream is coming true — in magnificent venues, supported by hundreds of millions of new Chinese winter sport fans.

You the Olympic athletes — you will show how the world would look like, if we all respect the same rules and each other.

Over the next two weeks you will compete with each other for the highest prize. At the same time, you will live peacefully together under one roof in the Olympic Village. There — there will be no discrimination for any reason whatsoever.

In our fragile world, where division, conflict and mistrust are on the rise, we show the world: Yes, it is possible to be fierce rivals, while at the same time living peacefully and respectfully together.

This is the mission of the Olympic Games: bringing us together in peaceful competition; always building bridges, never erecting walls; uniting humankind in all our diversity.

This mission is strongly supported by the United Nations General Assembly. It adopted the Olympic Truce Resolution by consensus of all 193 UN Member States. The resolution explicitly mentions you, the Olympic athletes, welcoming how you promote peace and human understanding through the Olympic ideal.

In this Olympic spirit of peace, I appeal to all political authorities across the world: Observe your commitment to this Olympic Truce. Give peace a chance.

Dear athletes, we all are standing with you. We all are supporting you. We all are cheering you on.

May this encourage you to go faster, to aim higher, (to) become stronger — together. In this way you will inspire the world in this Olympic Year with the same ambition, courage and strength like the Year of the Tiger.

3）Procrastination

练习说明：

1. This is a TED Talk speech in which the speaker shares his view about what procrastination is like to him, and elaborates on two kinds of procrastination. Brainstorm before interpreting: What is procrastination? In your opinion, what causes people to procrastinate, and what are the reasons behind procrastination? Do you have any advice to procrastinators?
2. The speaker's language is informal and easy, laughable in a light tone. As an interpreter, you should pay attention to the way he speaks.
3. The speech is divided into 15 segments. Record your interpretation at each stop signal.
4. After interpreting,
   1) review your recording for quality: Did your voice sound clear and understandable? Does your interpretation contain any language fillers, pauses longer than three seconds, disorganized information, or unidiomatic expressions?
   2) imagine you are his on-site interpreter and think about the following questions: How would you interpret for such a skillful public speaker? What are the potential challenges? How would you manage your paralanguage and kinesics to coordinate with his facial expressions, body language, pauses, and visual aids? How do you deal with laughter from the audience?

So in college, I was a government major, which means I had to write a lot of papers. Now, when a normal student writes a paper, they might spread the work out a little like THIS.

So, you know, you get started maybe a little slowly, but you get enough done in the first week (so) that — with some heavier days later on — everything gets done. Things stay civil. And I would want to do that like THAT. That would be the Plan. I would have it all ready to go, but then, actually, the paper would come along, and then I would kind of do THIS. And that would happen every single paper.

But then came my 90-page senior thesis, a paper you're supposed to spend a year on. And I knew for a paper like that, my normal work flow was not an option. It was way too big a project. So I planned things out, and I decided I kind of had to ~~go~~ (do) something like THIS. This is how the year would go. So I'd start off light, and I'd bump it up in the middle months, and then at the end, I would kick it up into high ~~gears~~ [gear], like a little staircase. How hard could it be to walk up the stairs? No big deal, right?

But then, the funniest thing happened. Those first few months? They came and went, and I couldn't quite do stuff. So we had an awesome new revised Plan. And then those middle months actually went by, and I didn't really write words, and so we were here. And then two months turned into one month, which turned into two weeks. And one day I woke up with three days until the deadline, still not having written a word, and so I did the only thing I could: I wrote 90 pages over 72 hours, pulling not one but two all-nighters — humans are not supposed to pull two all-nighters — sprinted across campus, dove in slow motion, and got it in just at the deadline.

I thought that was the end of everything. But a week later I get a call, and it's the school. And they say, "Is this Tim Urban?" And I say, "Yeah." And they say, "We need to talk about your thesis." And I say, "OK." And they say, "It's the best one we've ever seen." That did not happen. It was a very, very bad thesis. I just wanted to enjoy that one moment when all of you thought, "This guy is amazing!" No, no, it was very, very bad.

Anyway, today I'm a writer-blogger guy. I write the blog "Wait But Why." And a couple of years ago, I decided to write about procrastination. My behavior has always perplexed the non-procrastinators around me, and I wanted to explain to the non-procrastinators of the world what goes on in the heads of procrastinators, and why we are the way we are.

Now, I had a hypothesis that ~~did~~ the brains of procrastinators were actually different than the brains of other people. And to test this, I found an MRI lab that actually let me scan both my brain and the brain of a proven non-procrastinator, so I could compare them. I actually brought them here to show you today. I want you to take a look carefully to see if you can notice a difference.

I know that if you're not a trained brain expert, it's not that obvious, but just take a look, OK? So here's the brain of a non-procrastinator.

Now ... here's my brain. There is a difference. Both brains have a Rational Decision-Maker in them, but the procrastinator's brain also has an Instant Gratification Monkey. Now, what does this mean for the procrastinator? Well, it means everything's fine until this happens:

(a picture showing a dialog between two characters)
[This is a perfect time to get some work done.] [Nope!]

So the Rational Decision-Maker will make the rational decision to do something productive, but the Monkey doesn't like that Plan, so he actually takes the wheel, and he says, "Actually, let's read the entire Wikipedia page of the Nancy Kerrigan/Tonya Harding scandal, because I just remembered that that happened."

Then we're going to go over to the fridge, to see if there's anything new in there since 10 minutes ago. After that, we're going to go on a YouTube spiral that starts with videos of Richard Feynman talking about magnets and ends much, much later with us watching interviews with a popular singer's mom. "All of that's going to take a while, so we're not going to really have room on the schedule for any work today. Sorry!"

Now, what is going on here? The Instant Gratification Monkey does not seem like a guy you want behind the wheel. He lives entirely in the present moment. He has no memory of the past, no knowledge of the future, and he only cares about two things: easy and fun. Now, in the animal world, that works fine. If you're a dog and you spend your whole life doing nothing other than easy and fun things, you're a huge success!

And to the Monkey, humans are just another animal species. You have to keep well-slept, well-fed and propagating into the next generation, which in tribal times might have worked OK. But, if you haven't noticed, now we're not in tribal times. We're in an advanced civilization, and the Monkey does not know what that is, which is why we have another guy in our brain, the Rational Decision-Maker, who gives us the ability to do things no other animal can do. We can visualize the future. We can see the big picture. We can make long-term Plans. And he wants to take all of that into account. And he wants to just have us do whatever makes sense to be doing right now.

Now, sometimes it makes sense to be doing things that are easy and fun, like when you're having dinner or going to bed or enjoying well-earned leisure time. That's why there's an overlap. Sometimes they agree.

But other times, it makes much more sense to be doing things that are harder and less pleasant, for the sake of the big picture. And that's when we have a conflict. And for the procrastinator, that conflict tends to end a certain way every time, leaving him spending a lot of time in this orange zone, an easy and fun Place that's entirely out of the Makes-Sense circle. I call it the Dark Playground.

Now, the Dark Playground is a Place that all of you procrastinators out there know very well. It's where leisure activities happen at times when leisure activities are not supposed to be happening. The fun you have in the Dark Playground isn't actually fun, because it's completely unearned, and the air is filled with guilt, dread, anxiety, self-hatred — all those good procrastinator feelings. And the question is, in this situation, with the Monkey behind the wheel, how does the procrastinator ever get himself over here to this blue zone, a less pleasant Place, but where really important things happen?

Well, (it) turns out that the procrastinator has a guardian angel, someone who is always looking down on him and watching over him in his darkest moments — someone called the Panic Monster.

Now, the Panic Monster is dormant most of the time, but he suddenly wakes up anytime a deadline gets too close or there's danger of public embarrassment, a career disaster or some other scary consequence. And importantly, he's the only thing that the Monkey is terrified of. Now, he became very relevant in my life pretty recently, because the people of TED reached out to me about six months ago and invited me to do a TED Talk. Now, of course, I said yes. It's always been a dream of mine to have done a TED Talk in the past.

But in the middle of all this excitement, the Rational Decision-Maker seemed to have something else on his mind. He was saying, "Are we clear on what we just accepted? Do we get what's going to be now happening one day in the future? We need to sit down and work on this right now." And the Monkey said, "Totally agree, but ~~also~~ let's just open Google Earth and zoom in to the bottom of India, like 200 feet above the ground, and scroll up for two and a half hours until we get to the top of the country, so we can get a better feel for India." So that's what we did that day.

As six months turned into four and then two and then one, the people of TED decided to release the speakers. And I opened up the website, and there was my face staring right back at me. And guess who woke up?

So the Panic Monster starts losing his mind, and a few seconds later, the whole system's in mayhem. And the Monkey — remember, he's terrified of the Panic Monster — boom, he's up the tree! And finally, finally, the Rational Decision-Maker can take the wheel and I can start working on the talk.

Now, the Panic Monster explains all kinds of pretty insane procrastinator behavior, like how someone like me could spend two weeks unable to start the opening sentence of a paper, and then miraculously find the unbelievable work ethic to stay up all night and write eight pages. And this entire situation, with the three characters — this is the procrastinator's system. It's not pretty, but in the end, it works.

And this is what I decided to write about on the blog just a couple of years ago. Now when I did, I was amazed by the response. Literally thousands of emails came in, from all different kinds of people from all over the world, doing all different kinds of things. These are people who were nurses, bankers, painters, engineers and lots and lots of PhD students. And they were all writing, saying the same thing: "I have this problem too." But what struck me was the contrast between the light tone of the post and the heaviness of these emails. These people were writing with intense frustration about what procrastination had done to their lives, about what this Monkey had done to them. And I thought about this, and I said, well, if the procrastinator's system works, then what's going on? Why are all of these people in such a dark Place?

Well, it turns out that there's two kinds of procrastination. Everything I've talked about today, the examples I've given, they all have deadlines. When there are deadlines, the effects of procrastination are contained to the short term because the Panic Monster gets involved.

But there's a second kind of procrastination that happens in situations when there is no deadline. So if you wanted a career where you're a self-starter — something in the arts, something entrepreneurial — there's no deadlines on those things at first, because nothing's happening first, not until you've gone out and done the hard work to get some momentum, to get things going. There is [are] also all kinds of important things outside of your career that don't involve any deadlines, like seeing your family or exercising and taking care of your health, working on your relationship or getting out of a relationship that isn't working.

Now if the procrastinator's only mechanism of doing these hard things is the Panic Monster, that's a problem, because in all of these non-deadline situations, the Panic Monster doesn't show up. He has nothing to wake up for, so the effects of procrastination … they're not contained; they just extend outward forever.

And it's this long-term kind of procrastination that's much less visible and much less talked about than the funnier, short-term deadline-based kind. It's usually suffered quietly and privately. And it can be the source of a huge amount of long-term unhappiness, and regrets. And I thought, you know, that's why these people are emailing, and that's why they're in such a bad place. It's not that they're cramming for some project. It's that long-term procrastination has made them feel like a spectator, at times, in their own lives. You know, the frustration is not that they couldn't achieve their dreams; it's that they weren't even able to start chasing them.

So I read these emails and I had a little bit of an epiphany — that I don't think non-procrastinators exist. That's right — I think all of you are procrastinators. Now, you might not all be a mess, like some of us, and some of you may have a healthy relationship with deadlines, but remember: The Monkey's sneakiest trick is when the deadlines aren't there.

Now, I want to show you one last thing. I call this a Life Calendar. That's one box for every week of a 90-year life. That's not that many boxes, especially since we've already used a bunch of those. So I think we need to all take a long, hard look at that calendar. We need to think about what we're really procrastinating on, because everyone is procrastinating on something in life. We need to stay aware of the Instant Gratification Monkey. That's a job for all of us. And because there's not that many boxes on there, it's a job that should probably start today. Well, maybe not today, but … you know, sometime soon. Thank you.

五、补充阅读

1）雷天放，陈菁. 口译教程 [M]. 上海：上海外语教育出版社，2006.

2）卢信朝. 英汉口译技能教程：口译 [M]. 北京：旅游教育出版社，2009.

3）仲伟合. 英语口译基础教程 [M]. 北京：高等教育出版社，2007.

第13章 ▶ 表达中的应对

一、技能解说

1）口译是一场危机管理。无论译员准备如何充分，都可能由于认知处理能力有限、精力分配不当、主题知识不够等导致犯错，可以适当采取应对策略，尽量减少错误带来的影响。

2）常见的应对策略包括：

✓ 重组（reconstructing）：找一种"不算准确，但也不算错"的说法应对，之后再找机会"不动声色"地弥补；

✓ 重复（repetition）：通过重复发音或换词的办法争取思考时间，以便更好地表达；

✓ 省略（omission）：保主要信息，省略次要信息；

✓ 增译（addition）：解释某些专业词汇、术语或文化差异等，或明示逻辑关系等；

✓ 询问（asking）：万不得已可以现场求助讲话者。

3）牢记口译活动不是教室学习，口译目的是促成有效沟通。

初学者常常听到什么就译什么，结果是非但译不完整，而且输出急促、断断续续且不连贯。零碎信息过多反而影响听众理解，不如少说一点，但逻辑清楚、表达清晰。少说一点虽丢失了部分信息，但可能更容易让听众听懂。信息丢失导致的量上的变化，因效果的增强而抵消了。

二、训练方法

● 一词或一句多译的练习。小组练习，对同一句源语，每个同伴都给出意思一样但表达不同的译语。

● 收集英文长句，总结可行的译法，反思译得不好的原因。

● 小组练习口译并录像，练习站起来做口译。将自评与他评相结合，评价内容包括译语准确度与完整度、表达、眼神、肢体语言或动作、表情等。

三、练习案例点评

─────────────── 案例1 ───────────────

源　　语：You might never fail on the scale I did, but some failure in life is inevitable. It is impossible to live without failing at something, unless you live so cautiously that you might as well not have lived at all — in which case, you fail by default.

Failure gave me an inner security that I had never attained by passing examinations. Failure taught me things about myself that I could have learned no other way. I discovered that I had a strong will, and more discipline than I had suspected; I also found out that I had friends whose value was truly above the price of rubies.

The knowledge that you have emerged wiser and stronger from setbacks means that you are, ever after, secure in your ability to survive. You will never truly know yourself, or the strength of your relationships, until both have been tested by adversity. Such knowledge is a true gift, for all that it is painfully won, and it has been worth more than any qualification I ever earned.

学生译语: 或许你们从来没有像我这样失败过,但是人生中,失败是不可避免的。你的人生中不可能没有失败,除非你十分谨小慎微,就像你从来没有活过那样。失败给了一种内在世界的安宁,这是考试通过无法给予我的。失败教会了我很多东西,让我明白了一些我不可能通过别的途径明白的道理。在失败中,我发现我拥有强壮的意志和比我想象中更自律的精神,我还有朋友。你的知识、你自身和情感关系是只有在逆境中才能……嗯……体现出来的,所以说失败其实是一种礼物,比任何资质都来得更实在。

📋 点评

1)译语大意是对的,细节也比较完整,表达基本流畅。

2)罗琳的这篇演讲是精心准备的,句子结构都比较复杂,风格正式、有文学色彩,长句、难词比较多,语速又比较快,还有双重否定句、插入语、暗喻等,不容易听懂并抓住意思,笔记也可能记不下多少,遗漏难以避免,只能尽力译出大意,风格优美就不强求了。可以吃透原文解决语言障碍之后,过一段时间再来练口译。

3)"除非你十分谨小慎微,就像你从来没有活过那样"是没有理解源语只按字面的翻译;但"失败给了一种内在世界的安宁,这是考试通过无法给予我的。失败教会了我很多东西,让我明白了一些我不可能通过别的途径明白的道理"这是理解以后的译语,虽然还有一点小瑕疵,但至少意义清晰明确,且比较符合中文表达习惯。

3)每句都有"你",去掉后更符合中文表达习惯。

4)Whose value was truly above rubies没有直译,而是处理为"我还有朋友",这也是一种不错的应对手段。

5）"你的知识、你自身和情感关系是只有在逆境中才能……嗯……体现出来的，所以说失败其实是一种礼物，比任何资质都来得更实在"有较多信息遗漏，可能的原因之一是源语信息密集。建议大部分用脑记分析处理，可使信息记忆更完整。

教师评分：85。

案例2

源　　语：So for any of us in this room today, let's start out by admitting we're lucky. We don't live in the world our mothers lived in, our grandmothers lived in, where career choices for women were so limited. And if you're in this room today, most of us grew up in a world where we had basic civil rights, and amazingly, we still live in a world where some women don't have them. But all that aside, we still have a problem, and it's a real problem. And the problem is this: Women are not making it to the top of any profession anywhere in the world. The numbers tell the story quite clearly. A hundred and ninety heads of state — nine are women. Of all the people in parliament in the world, 13 percent are women. In the corporate sector, women at the top, C-level jobs, board seats — tops out at 15, 16 percent. The numbers have not moved since 2002 and are going in the wrong direction. And even in the non-profit world, a world we sometimes think of as being led by more women, women at the top: 20 percent.

学生译语：在座的各位，首先，我们得承认自己是幸运的。我们没有生活在我们母亲，或者我们祖母生活的世界里，那时女性的职业选择十分有限。在座的各位基本都成长在一个拥有着基本公民权的世界里，然而，令人惊讶的是，有些女性仍没办法享受这些权利。除此之外，我们还面临着另一个问题，而这个问题也是实实在在存在的，即在世界上任何一个地方，女性没法成为各自领域里的领导者。二者是有数据支撑的。一百九十位国家元首中，有九位是女性。在各国议会的成员中，百分之十三是女性。在企业部门，女性在高层和董事会席位的占比为百分之十五到百分之十六。2002年以来，这些数值、占比也并没有提高，甚至朝着反方向下降。即使是在非营利的领域，一个我们认为由更多女性来领导的领域，占比也不超过百分之二十。

点评

1）内容译得较完整，表达虽有些啰嗦，但比较流畅、地道。虽然源语速度较快，但译者应对较好。

2）"那时女性的职业选择十分有限""令人惊讶的是，有些女性仍没办法享受这些权利"等表达都比较灵活准确。

3）译语中也存在一些问题。"即在世界上任何一个地方，女性没法成

为各自领域里的领导者"语义模糊；"二者是有数据支撑的"中的"二者"指代不明；"我们没有生活在我们母亲，或者我们祖母生活的世界里"中的后两个"我们"冗余；women at the top, C-level jobs, board seats罗列三项中第二项C-level jobs漏译。

教师评分：90。

四、篇章练习

生词表

英文	中文
testicles	睾丸
testosterone	睾酮
memory circuits	记忆电路
sleep deprivation	睡眠剥夺
slumber	睡眠
MRI scanner	核磁共振扫描仪
snapshot	快照
hippocampus	海马体
electrode	电极
silver lining	（不幸中的）一线希望
elixir	灵丹妙药，长生不老药
cartoon anvil	卡通铁砧（卡通动画或漫画中常见的砸头铁砧，用以表现夸张或幽默效果）
agoraphobia	陌生环境恐惧症
collude with	密谋
apathy	冷漠，无动于衷
Plutarch	普鲁塔克（罗马帝国时期的希腊作家）
bio break	（为上厕所等生理需求准备的）会间小憩
senior exec	高级主管
pre-med	医学院预科生
Hegelian dialectic	黑格尔辩证法
venture capitalist	风险投资人
maternity leave	产假
gas pedal	油门

1）Sleep is your superpower

练习说明:

1. This is a talk about sleep given by a brain scientist, titled "Sleep Is Your Superpower." Brainstorm before listening: What will the speaker talk about and how? Do you expect any difficulties in interpreting, e.g., names, numbers, terms, lists, etc., and how would you cope with them?

2. The talk is divided into 18 segments. Record a video of your interpretation at each stop signal.

3. After interpreting,

   1) review your recording for quality: Does your interpretation contain any language fillers, pauses longer than three seconds, disorganized information, or unidiomatic expressions?

   2) think about the following questions:

   • Did your note serve as a backup of your memory? Did you look good and sound good when interpreting? Why or why not?

   • Do you have any difficulties in rephrasing the message? What are the specific difficulties and how did you cope with them when interpreting? Share and discuss with your peers.

Thank you very much. Well, I would like to start with testicles. Men who sleep five hours a night have significantly smaller testicles than those who sleep seven hours or more. In addition, men who routinely sleep just four to five hours a night will have a level of testosterone which is that of someone 10 years their senior. So a lack of sleep will age a man by a decade in terms of that critical aspect of wellness. And we see equivalent impairments in female reproductive health caused by a lack of sleep. This is the best news that I have for you today.

From this point, it may only get worse. Not only will I tell you about the wonderfully good things that happen when you get sleep, but the alarmingly bad things that happen when you don't get enough, both for your brain and for your body.

Let me start with the brain and the functions of learning and memory, because what we've discovered over the past 10 or so years is that you need sleep after learning to essentially hit the save button on those new memories so that you don't forget. But recently, we discovered that you also need sleep before learning to actually prepare your brain, almost like a dry sponge ready to initially soak up new information. And without sleep, the memory circuits of the brain essentially become waterlogged, as it were, and you can't absorb new memories.

So let me show you the data. Here in this study, we decided to test the hypothesis that pulling the all-nighter was a good idea. So we took a group of individuals and we assigned them to one of two experimental groups: a sleep group and a sleep deprivation group. Now the sleep group — they're going to get a full eight hours of slumber, but the deprivation group — we're going to keep them awake in the laboratory, under full supervision. There's no naps or caffeine, by the way, so it's miserable for everyone involved. And then the next day, we're going to place those participants inside an MRI scanner and we're going to have them try and learn a whole list of new facts as we're taking snapshots of brain activity. And then we're going to test them to see how effective that learning has been. And when you put those two groups head-to-head, what you find is a quite significant, 40 percent deficit in the ability of the brain to make new memories without sleep.

I think this should be concerning, considering what we know is happening to sleep in our education populations right now. In fact, to put that in context, it would be the difference in a child acing an exam versus failing it miserably — 40 percent. And we've gone on to discover what goes wrong within your brain to produce these types of learning disabilities. And there's a structure that sits on the left and the right side of your brain, called the hippocampus. And you can think of the hippocampus almost like the informational inbox of your brain. It's very good at receiving new memory files and then holding on to them. And when you look at this structure in those people who'd had a full night of sleep, we saw lots of healthy learning-related activity. Yet in those people who were sleep-deprived, we actually couldn't find any significant signal whatsoever. So it's almost as though sleep deprivation had shut down your memory inbox, and any new incoming files — they were just being bounced. You couldn't effectively commit new experiences to memory.

So that's the bad that can happen if I were to take sleep away from you, but let me just come back to that control group for a second. Do you remember those folks that got a full eight hours of sleep? Well, we can ask a very different question: What is it about the physiological quality of your sleep when you do get it that restores and enhances your memory and learning ability each and every day? And by placing electrodes all over the head, what we've discovered is that there are big, powerful brainwaves that happen during the very deepest stages of sleep that have riding on top of them spectacular bursts of electrical activity that we call sleep spindles. And it's the combined quality of these deep-sleep brainwaves that acts like a file-transfer mechanism at night, shifting memories from a short-term vulnerable reservoir to a more permanent long-term storage site within the brain, and therefore protecting them, making them safe. And it is important that we understand what during sleep actually transacts these memory benefits, because there are real medical and societal implications.

And let me just tell you about one area that we've moved this work out into, clinically, which is the context of aging and dementia. Because it's of course no secret that, as we get older, our learning and memory abilities begin to fade and decline. But what we've also discovered is that a physiological signature of aging is that your sleep gets worse, especially that deep quality of sleep that I was just discussing. And only last year, we finally published evidence that these two things, they're not simply co-occurring, they are significantly interrelated. And it suggests that the disruption of deep sleep is an underappreciated factor that is contributing to cognitive decline or memory decline in aging, and most recently we've discovered, in Alzheimer's disease as well.

Now, I know this is remarkably depressing news. It's in the mail. It's coming at you. But there's a potential silver lining here. Unlike many of the other factors that we know are associated with aging, for example changes in the physical structure of the brain, ~~that's~~ (which is) fiendishly difficult to treat, ~~but~~ that sleep is a missing piece in the explanatory puzzle of aging and Alzheimer's is exciting because we may be able to do something about it.

And one way that we are approaching this at my sleep center is not by using sleeping pills, by the way. Unfortunately, they are blunt instruments that do not produce naturalistic sleep. Instead, we're actually developing a method based on this. It's called direct current brain stimulation. You insert a small amount of voltage into the brain, so small you typically don't feel it, but it has a measurable impact. Now if you apply this stimulation during sleep in young, healthy adults, as if you're sort of singing in time with those deep-sleep brainwaves, not only can you amplify the size of those deep-sleep brainwaves, but in doing so, we can almost double the amount of memory benefit that you get from sleep. The question now is whether we can translate this same affordable, potentially portable piece of technology into older adults and those with dementia. Can we restore back some healthy quality of deep sleep, and in doing so, can we salvage aspects of their learning and memory function? That is my real hope now. That's one of our moon-shot goals, as it were.

So that's an example of sleep for your brain, but sleep is just as essential for your body. We've already spoken about sleep loss and your reproductive system. Or I could tell you about sleep loss and your cardiovascular system, and that all it takes is one hour. Because there is a global experiment performed on 1.6 billion people across 70 countries twice a year, and it's called Daylight ~~Savings~~ [Saving] Time. Now, in the spring, when we lose one hour of sleep, we see a subsequent 24 percent increase in heart attacks that following day. In the autumn, when we gain an hour of sleep, we see a 21 percent reduction in heart attacks. Isn't that incredible? And you see exactly the same profile for car crashes, road traffic accidents, even suicide rates.

But as a deeper dive, I want to focus on this: sleep loss and your immune system. And here, I'll introduce natural killer cells, and you can think of natural killer cells almost like the secret service agents of your immune system. They are very good at identifying dangerous, unwanted elements and eliminating them. So what you wish for is a virile set of these immune assassins at all times, and tragically, that's what you don't have if you're not sleeping enough.

So here in this experiment, you're not going to have your sleep deprived for an entire night, you're simply going to have your sleep restricted to four hours for one single night, and then we're going to look to see what's the percent reduction in immune cell activity that you suffer. And it's not small — it's not 10 percent, it's not 20 percent. There was a 70 percent drop in natural killer cell activity. That's a concerning state of immune deficiency, and you can perhaps understand why we're now finding significant links between short sleep duration and your risk for the development of numerous forms of cancer. Currently, that list includes cancer of the bowel, cancer of the prostate and cancer of the breast. In fact, the link between a lack of sleep and cancer is now so strong that the World Health Organization has classified any form of nighttime shift work as a probable carcinogen, because of a disruption of your sleep-wake rhythms.

So you may have heard of that old maxim that you can sleep when you're dead. Well, I'm being quite serious now — it is mortally unwise advice. We know this from epidemiological studies across millions of individuals. There's a simple truth: The shorter your sleep, the shorter your life. Short sleep predicts all-cause mortality.

And if increasing your risk for the development of cancer or even Alzheimer's disease were not sufficiently disquieting, we have since discovered that a lack of sleep will even erode the very fabric of biological life itself, your DNA genetic code. So here in this study, they took a group of healthy adults and they limited them to six hours of sleep a night for one week, and then they measured the change in their gene activity profile relative to when those same individuals were getting a full eight hours of sleep a night. And there were two critical findings. First, a sizable and significant 711 genes were distorted in their activity, caused by a lack of sleep. The second result was that about half of those genes were actually increased in their activity. The other half were decreased.

Now those genes that were switched off by a lack of sleep were genes associated with your immune system, so once again, you can see that immune deficiency. In contrast, those genes that were actually upregulated or increased by way of a lack of sleep, were genes associated with the promotion of tumors, genes associated with long-term chronic inflammation within the body, and genes associated with stress, and, as a consequence, cardiovascular disease. There is simply no aspect of your wellness that can retreat at the sign of sleep deprivation and get away unscathed. It's rather like a broken water pipe in your home. Sleep loss will leak down into every nook and cranny of your physiology, even tampering with the very DNA nucleic alphabet that spells out your daily health narrative.

And at this point, you may be thinking, "Oh my goodness, how do I start to get better sleep? What are your tips for good sleep?" Well, beyond avoiding the damaging and harmful impact of alcohol and caffeine on sleep, and if you're struggling with sleep at night, avoiding naps during the day, I have two pieces of advice for you.

The first is regularity. Go to bed at the same time, wake up at the same time, no matter whether it's the weekday or the weekend. Regularity is king, and it will anchor your sleep and improve the quantity and the quality of that sleep. The second is keep it cool. Your body needs to drop its core temperature by about two to three degrees Fahrenheit to initiate sleep and then to stay asleep, and it's the reason you will always find it easier to fall asleep in a room that's too cold than too hot. So aim for a bedroom temperature of around 65 degrees, or about 18 degrees Celsius. That's going to be optimal for the sleep of most people.

And then finally — in taking a step back — then, what is the mission-critical statement here? Well, I think it may be this: Sleep, unfortunately, is not an optional lifestyle luxury. Sleep is a nonnegotiable biological necessity. It is your life-support system, and it is Mother Nature's best effort yet at immortality. And the decimation of sleep throughout industrialized nations is having a catastrophic impact on our health, our wellness, even the safety and the education of our children. It's a silent sleep loss epidemic, and it is fast becoming one of the greatest public health challenges that we face in the 21st century.

I believe it is now time for us to reclaim our right to a full night of sleep, and without embarrassment or that unfortunate stigma of laziness. And in doing so, we can be reunited with the most powerful elixir of life, the Swiss Army knife of health, as it were. And with that soapbox rant over, I will simply say, good night, good luck, and above all … I do hope you sleep well. Thank you very much indeed.

2）The fringe benefits of failure, and the importance of imagination

练习说明：

1. These are excerpts of J. K. Rowling's commencement address at Harvard University in 2008. In the speech, she talked about her life after graduation from college. Brainstorm before listening: What do you think she would talk about, and how? What may cause difficulties for interpreting this speech?
2. The excerpts are divided into 16 segments. Interpret the message at each stop signal and record a video of your interpreting.

3. After interpreting,
   1) review your recording for quality: Did you get the correct message? Does your interpretation contain any language fillers, pauses longer than three seconds, disorganized information, or unidiomatic expressions?
   2) think about the following questions: Did you encounter any difficulties during interpreting such as struggling to find proper expressions in Chinese, forgetting the names of people or places, being unfamiliar with terms in *Harry Potter*, grappling with long sentences? How did you cope with them? Share and discuss with your peers.

President Faust,

Members of the Harvard Corporation and the Board of Overseers,

Members of the faculty,

Proud parents, and, above all, graduates,

The first thing I would like to say is "Thank you." Not only has Harvard given me an extraordinary honor, but the weeks of fear and nausea I have endured at the thought of giving this commencement address have made me lose weight. A win-win situation! Now all I have to do is take deep breaths, squint at the red banners and convince myself that I am at the world's largest Gryffindors' reunion.

Delivering a commencement address is a great responsibility; or so I thought until I cast my mind back to my own graduation. The commencement speaker that day was the distinguished British philosopher Baroness Mary Warnock. Reflecting on her speech has helped me enormously in writing this one, because it turns out that I can't remember a single word she said. This liberating discovery enables me to proceed without any fear that I might inadvertently influence you to abandon promising careers in business, the law, or politics for the giddy delights of becoming a gay wizard.

You see? If all you remember in years to come is the "gay wizard" joke, I've come out ahead of Baroness Mary Warnock. Achievable goals — the first step to self-improvement.

Actually, I have wracked my mind and heart for what I ought to say to you today. I have asked myself what I wish I had known at my own graduation, and what important lessons I have learned in the 21 years that have expired between that day and this.

I have come up with two answers. On this wonderful day when we are gathered together to celebrate your academic success, I have decided to talk to you about the benefits of failure. And as you stand on the threshold of what is sometimes called "real life," I want to extol the crucial importance of imagination.

These may seem quixotic or paradoxical choices, but bear with me.

Looking back at the twenty-one-year-old that I was at graduation, is a slightly uncomfortable experience for the forty-two-year-old that she has become. Half my lifetime ago, I was striking an uneasy balance between the ambition I had for myself, and what those closest to me expected of me.

I was convinced that the only thing I wanted to do, ever, was (to) write novels. However, my parents, both of whom came from impoverished backgrounds and neither of whom had been to college, took the view that my overactive imagination was an amusing personal quirk that could never pay a mortgage, or secure a pension.

I know the irony strikes with the force of a cartoon anvil now, but …

So they hoped that I would take a vocational degree; I wanted to study English Literature. A compromise was reached that in retrospect satisfied nobody, and I went up to study Modern Languages. Hardly had my parents' car rounded the corner at the end of the road than I ditched German and scuttled off down the Classics corridor.

I cannot remember telling my parents that I was studying Classics; they might well have found out for the first time on graduation day. Of all the subjects on this planet, I think they would have been hard put to name one less useful than Greek mythology when it came to securing the keys to an executive bathroom.

Now, I would like to make it clear, in parentheses, that I do not blame my parents for their point of view. There is an expiry date on blaming your parents for steering you in the wrong direction; the moment you are old enough to take the wheel, responsibility lies with you. What is more, I cannot criticize my parents for hoping that I would never experience poverty. They had been poor themselves, and I have since been poor, and I quite agree with them that it is not an ennobling experience. Poverty entails fear, and stress, and sometimes depression; it means a thousand petty humiliations and hardships. Climbing out of poverty by your own efforts — that is something on which to pride yourself, but poverty itself is romanticized only by fools.

What I feared most for myself at your age was not poverty, but failure.

At your age, in spite of a distinct lack of motivation at university, where I had spent far too long in the coffee bar writing stories, and far too little time at lectures, I had a knack for passing examinations, and that, for years, had been the measure of success in my life and that of my peers.

I am not dull enough to suppose that because you are young, gifted and well-educated, you have never known heartbreak, hardship or heartache. Talent and intelligence never yet inoculated anyone against the caprice of the Fates, and I do not for a moment suppose that everyone here has enjoyed an existence of unruffled privilege and contentment.

However, the fact that you are graduating from Harvard suggests that you are not very well-acquainted with failure. You might be driven by a fear of failure quite as much as a desire for success. Indeed, your conception of failure might not be too far a move from the average person's idea of success, so high have you already flown.

Ultimately, we all have to decide for ourselves what constitutes failure, but the world is quite eager to give you a set of criteria if you let it. So I think it fair to say that by any conventional measure, a mere seven years after my graduation day, I had failed on an epic scale. An exceptionally short-lived marriage had imploded, and I was jobless, a lone parent, and as poor as it is possible to be in modern Britain without being homeless. The fears that my parents had had for me, and that I had had for myself, had both come to pass, and by every usual standard, I was the biggest failure I knew.

Now, I am not going to stand here and tell you that failure is fun. That period of my life was a dark one, and I had no idea that there was going to be what the press has since represented as a kind of fairy tale resolution. I had no idea then how far the tunnel extended, and for a long time, any light at the end of it was a hope rather than a reality.

So why do I talk about the benefits of failure? Simply because failure meant a stripping away of the inessential. I stopped pretending to myself that I was anything other than what I was, and began to direct all my energy into finishing the only work that mattered to me. Had I really succeeded at anything else, I might never have found the determination to succeed in the one arena where I believed I truly belonged. I was set free, because my greatest fear had been realized, and I was still alive, and I still had a daughter whom I adored, and I had an old typewriter and a big idea. And so rock bottom became the solid foundation on which I rebuilt my life.

You might never fail on the scale I did, but some failure in life is inevitable. It is impossible to live without failing at something, unless you live so cautiously that you might as well not have lived at all — in which case, you fail by default.

Failure gave me an inner security that I had never attained by passing examinations. Failure taught me things about myself that I could have learned no other way. I discovered that I had a strong will, and more discipline than I had suspected; I also found out that I had friends whose value was truly above the price of rubies.

The knowledge that you have emerged wiser and stronger from setbacks means that you are, ever after, secure in your ability to survive. You will never truly know yourself, or the strength of your relationships, until both have been tested by adversity. Such knowledge is a true gift, for all that it is painfully won, and it has been worth more than any qualification I ever earned.

So given a Time Turner, I would tell my 21-year-old self that personal happiness lies in knowing that life is not a check-list of acquisition or achievement. Your qualifications, your CV, are not your life, though you will meet many people of my age and older who confuse the two. Life is difficult, and complicated, and beyond anyone's total control, and the humility to know that will enable you to survive its vicissitudes.

Now you might think that I chose my second theme, the importance of imagination, because of the part it played in rebuilding my life, but that is not wholly so. Though I personally will defend the value of bedtime stories to my last gasp, I have learned to value imagination in a much broader sense. Imagination is not only the uniquely human capacity to envision that which is not, and therefore the fount of all invention and innovation. In its arguably most transformative and revelatory capacity, it is the power that enables us to empathize with humans whose experiences we have never shared. …

… Unlike any other creature on this planet, human beings can learn and understand, without having experienced. They can think themselves into other people's places.

Of course, this is a power, like my brand of fictional magic, that is morally neutral. One might use such an ability to manipulate, or control, just as much as to understand or sympathize.

And many prefer not to exercise their imaginations at all. They choose to remain comfortably within the bounds of their own experience, never troubling to wonder how it would feel to have been born other than they are. They can refuse to hear screams or peer inside cages; they can close their minds and hearts to any suffering that does not touch them personally; they can refuse to know.

I might be tempted to envy people who can live that way, except that I do not think they have any fewer nightmares than I do. Choosing to live in narrow spaces leads to a form of mental agoraphobia, and that brings its own terrors. I think the wilfully unimaginative see more monsters. They are often more afraid.

What is more, those who choose not to empathize enable real monsters. For without ever committing an act of outright evil ourselves, we collude with it, through our own apathy.

One of the many things I learned at the end of that Classics corridor down which I ventured at the age of 18, in search of something I could not then define, was this, written by the Greek author Plutarch: What we achieve inwardly will change outer reality.

That is an astonishing statement and yet proven a thousand times every day of our lives. It expresses, in part, our inescapable connection with the outside world, the fact that we touch other people's lives simply by existing.

But how much more are you, Harvard graduates of 2008, likely to touch other people's lives? Your intelligence, your capacity for hard work, the education you have earned and received, give you unique status, and unique responsibilities.

If you choose to use your status and influence to raise your voice on behalf of those who have no voice; if you choose to identify not only with the powerful, but with the powerless; if you retain the ability to imagine yourself into the lives of those who do not have your advantages, then it will not only be your proud families who celebrate your existence, but thousands and millions of people whose reality you have helped change. We do not need magic to transform our world, we carry all the power we need inside ourselves already: We have the power to imagine better.

I am nearly finished. I have one last hope for you, which is something that I already had at 21. The friends with whom I sat on graduation day have been my friends for life. They are my children's godparents, the people to whom I've been able to turn in times of real trouble, people who have been kind enough not to sue me when I took their names for Death Eaters. At our graduation we were bound by enormous affection, by our shared experience of a time that could never come again, and, of course, by the knowledge that we held certain photographic evidence that would be exceptionally valuable if any of us ran for Prime Minister.

So today, I wish you nothing better than similar friendships. And tomorrow, I hope that even if you remember not a single word of mine, you remember those of Seneca, another of those old Romans I met when I fled down the Classics corridor, in retreat from career ladders, in search of ancient wisdom: As is a tale, so is life: not how long it is, but how good it is, is what matters.

I wish you all very good lives. Thank you very much.

3）Why we have too few women leaders

练习说明：

1. This is a talk by former Facebook COO Sheryl Sandberg. In the talk, she looks at why there is a smaller percentage of women than men who reach the top of their professions, and offers three powerful pieces of advice to women aiming for the C-suite. Brainstorm before listening: In regard to this topic, can you predict the pieces of advice to women?

2. The talk is divided into 15 segments. Record your interpretation at each stop signal.

3. After interpreting,

   1) review your recording for quality: Did you get the correct message? Does your interpretation contain any language fillers, pauses longer than three seconds, disorganized information, or unidiomatic expressions?

   2) think about the following questions:

   • Did you encounter any difficulties in interpreting, such as the speaker talking too fast with intensified numbers, colloquial expressions, jokes? How did you cope with them?

   • Which aspects were the most challenging for you, such as understanding, memorizing, re-expressing? Why did you find them difficult? Share and discuss your experience with your peers.

So for any of us in this room today, let's start out by admitting we're lucky. We don't live in the world our mothers lived in, our grandmothers lived in, where career choices for women were so limited. And if you're in this room today, most of us grew up in (a) world where we had basic civil rights, and amazingly, we still live in a world where some women don't have them. But all that aside, we still have a problem, and it's a real problem. And the problem is this: Women are not making it to the top of any profession anywhere in the world. The numbers tell the story quite clearly. A hundred and ninety heads of state — nine are women. Of all the people in parliament in the world, 13 percent are women. In the corporate sector, women at the top, C-level jobs, board seats — tops out at 15, 16 percent. The numbers have not moved since 2002 and are going in the wrong direction. And even in the non-profit world, a world we sometimes think of as being led by more women, women at the top: 20 percent.

We also have another problem, which is that women face harder choices between professional success and personal fulfillment. A recent study in the U.S. showed that, of senior managers … of married senior managers, two-thirds of the married men had children and only one-third of the married women had children. A couple of years ago, I was in New York, and I was pitching a deal, and I was in one of those fancy New York private equity offices you can picture. And I'm in the meeting — it's about a three-hour meeting — and two hours in (the meeting), there's kind of

~~needs to be~~ [need for] that bio break, and everyone stands up, and the partner running the meeting starts looking really embarrassed. And I realize he doesn't know where the women's room is in his office. So I start looking around for moving boxes, figuring they just moved in, but I don't see any. And so I said, "So did you just move into this office?" And he said, "No, we've been here about a year." And I said, "Are you telling me that I am the only woman to have pitched a deal in this office in a year?" And he looked at me, and he said, "Yeah. Or maybe you're the only one who had to go to the bathroom."

So the question is, how are we going to fix this? How do we change these numbers at the top? How do we make this different? I want to start out by saying, I talk about this — about keeping women in the workforce — because I really think that's the answer. In the high-income part of our workforce, in the people who end up at the top — Fortune 500 CEO jobs, or the equivalent in other industries — the problem, I am convinced, is that women are dropping out. Now people talk about this a lot, and they talk about things like flextime and mentoring and programs companies should have to train women. I want to talk about none of that today, even though that's all really important. Today I want to focus on what we can do as individuals. What are the messages we need to tell ourselves? What are the messages we tell the women that work with and for us? What are the messages we tell our daughters?

Now, at the outset, I want to be very clear that this speech comes with no judgments. I don't have the right answer. I don't even have it for myself. I left San Francisco, where I live, on Monday, and I was getting on the plane for this conference. And my daughter, who's three, when I dropped her off at preschool, did that whole hugging-the-leg, crying "Mommy, don't get on the plane" thing. This is hard. I feel guilty sometimes. I know no women, whether they're at home or whether they're in the workforce, who don't feel that sometimes. So I'm not saying that staying in the workforce is the right thing for everyone.

My talk today is about what the messages are if you do want to stay in the workforce, and I think there are three. One, sit at the table. Two, make your partner a real partner. And three, don't leave before you leave. Number one: sit at the table. Just a couple weeks ago at Facebook, we hosted (a meeting for) a very senior government official, and he came in to meet with senior execs from around Silicon Valley. And everyone kind of sat at the table. And then he had these two women who were traveling with him who were pretty senior in his department, and I kind of said to them, "Sit at the table. Come, sit at the table," and they sat on the side of the room.

When I was in college my senior year, I took a course called European Intellectual History. Don't you love that kind of thing from college? I wish I could do that now. And I took it with my roommate, Carrie, who was then a brilliant literary student — and went on to be a brilliant literary scholar — and my brother — smart guy, but a water-polo-playing pre-med, who was a sophomore.

The three of us take this class together. And then Carrie reads all the books in the original Greek and Latin, goes to all the lectures. I read all the books in English and go to most of the lectures. My brother is kind of busy. He reads one book of 12 and goes to a couple of lectures, marches himself up to our room a couple days before the exam to get himself tutored. The three of us go to the exam together, and we sit down. And we studied … You know, sit there for three hours and [with] our little blue notebooks … Yes, I'm that old. And we walk out. We look at each other, and we say, "How did you do?" And Carrie says, "Boy, I feel like I didn't really draw out the main point on the Hegelian dialectic." And I say, "God, I really wish I had really connected John Locke's theory of property with the philosophers that follow." And my brother says, "I got the top grade in the class." "You got the top grade in the class? You don't know anything."

The problem with these stories is that they show what the data shows: Women systematically underestimate their own abilities. If you test men and women, and you ask them questions on totally objective criteria like GPAs, men get it wrong slightly high, and women get it wrong slightly low.

Women do not negotiate for themselves in the workforce. A study in the last two years of people entering the workforce out of college showed that 57 percent of boys entering — or men, I guess — are negotiating their first salary, and only seven percent of women (are doing the same). And most importantly, men attribute their success to themselves, and women attribute it to other external factors. If you ask men why they did a good job, they'll say, "I'm awesome. Obviously. Why are you even asking?" If you ask women why they did a good job, what they'll say is someone helped them, they got lucky, they worked really hard.

Why does this matter? Boy, it matters a lot because no one gets to the corner office by sitting on the side, not at the table, and no one gets the promotion if they don't think they deserve their success, or they don't even understand their own success.

I wish the answer were easy. I wish I could just go tell all the young women I work for, all these fabulous women, "Believe in yourself and negotiate for yourself. Own your own success." I wish I could tell that to my daughter. But it's not that simple. Because what the data shows, above all else, is one thing, which is that success and likeability are positively correlated for men and negatively correlated for women. And everyone's nodding, because we all know this to be true.

There's a really good study that shows this really well. There's a famous Harvard Business School study on a woman named Heidi Roizen. And she's a(n) operator in a venture capital, in a company in Silicon Valley, and she uses her contacts to become a very successful venture capitalist. In 2002, not so long ago, a professor who was then at Columbia University took that case and made it Heidi Roizen. And he gave the case out, both of them, to two groups of students. He changed exactly one word: "Heidi" to "Howard." But that one word made a really big difference. He then surveyed the students, and the good news was the students, both men and women, thought Heidi and Howard were equally competent, and that's good. The bad news was that everyone liked Howard. He's a great guy. You want to work for him. You want to spend the day fishing with him. But Heidi? Not so sure. She's a little out for herself. She's a little political. You're not sure you'd want to work for her.

This is the complication. We have to tell our daughter(s) and our colleagues, we have to tell ourselves to believe we got the "A," to reach for the promotion, to sit at the table, and we have to do it in a world where, for them, there are sacrifices they will make for that, even though for their brothers, there were [are] not.

The saddest thing about all of this is that it's really hard to remember this. And I'm about to tell a story which is truly embarrassing for me but I think important. I gave this talk at Facebook not so long ago to about 100 employees, and a couple hours later, there was a young woman who works there sitting kind of outside my little desk, and she wanted to talk to me. And I said "OK," and she sat down, and we talked. And she said, "I learned something today. I learned that I need to keep my hand up." I said, "What do you mean?" She said, "Well, you are [were] giving this talk, and then you said you are [were] going to take two more questions. And I had my hand up with lots of other people, and then you took two more questions. And I put my hand down, and I noticed all the women put their hand(s) down, and then you took more questions, only from the men." And I thought to myself, wow, if it's me who cares about this, obviously — giving this talk, during this talk, I can't even notice that the men's hands are still raised, and the women's hands are still raised — how good are we as managers of our companies and our organizations at seeing that the men are reaching for opportunities more than women? We've got to get women to sit at the table.

Message number two: Make your partner a real partner. I've become convinced that we've made more progress in the workforce than we have in the home. The data shows this very clearly. If a woman and a man work full-time and have a child, the woman does twice the amount of housework the man does, and the woman does three times the amount of childcare the man does. So she's got three jobs or two jobs, and he's got one. Who do you think drops out when someone needs to be home more? The causes of this are really complicated, and I don't have time to go into them. And I don't think Sunday football-watching and general laziness is the cause.

I think the cause is more complicated. I think, as a society, we put more pressure on our boys to succeed than we do on our girls. I know men that stay home and work in the home to support wives with careers, and it's hard. When I go to the Mommy-and-Me stuff and I see the father there, I notice that the other mommies don't play with him. And that's a problem, because we have to make it as important a job, because it's the hardest job in the world to work inside the home, for people of both genders, if we're going to even things out and let women stay in the workforce. Studies show that households with equal earning and equal responsibility also have half the divorce rate.

Message number three: Don't leave before you leave. I think there's a really deep irony to the fact that actions women are taking — and I see this all the time — with the objective of staying in the workforce actually lead to their eventually leaving. Here's what happens: We're all busy. Everyone's busy. A woman's busy. And she starts thinking about having a child, and from the moment she starts thinking about having a child, she starts thinking about making room for that child. "How am I going to fit this into everything else I'm doing?" And literally from that moment, she doesn't raise her hand anymore; she doesn't look for a promotion; she doesn't take on the new project; she doesn't say, "Me. I want to do that." She starts leaning back. The problem is that … let's say she got pregnant that day. That day — nine months of pregnancy, three months of maternity leave, six months to catch your breath — fast-forward two years. More often — and as I've seen it — women start thinking about this way earlier: when they get engaged, when they get married, when they start thinking about trying to have a child, which can take a long time. One woman came to see me about this, and I kind of looked at her — she looked a little young. And I said, "So are you and your husband thinking about having a baby?" And she said, "Oh no, I'm not married." She didn't even have a boyfriend. I said, "You're thinking about this just way too early."

But the point is that what happens once you start kind of quietly leaning back? Everyone who's been through this — and I'm here to tell you, once you have a child at home, your job better be really good to go back, because it's hard to leave that kid at home — your job needs to be challenging. It needs to be rewarding. You need to feel like you're making a difference. And if two years ago you didn't take a promotion and some guy next to you did, if three years ago you stopped looking for new opportunities, you're going to be bored because you should have kept your foot on the gas pedal.

Don't leave before you leave. Stay in. Keep your foot on the gas pedal, until the very day you need to leave to take a break for a child — and then make your decisions. Don't make decisions too far in advance, particularly ones you're not even conscious you're making.

My generation really, sadly, is not going to change the numbers at the top. They're just not moving. We're not gonna get to where 50 percent of the population … In my generation, there will not be 50 percent of ~~people~~ [women] at the top of any industry.

But I'm hopeful that future generations can. I think a world that was run where half of our countries and half of our companies were run by women, would be a better world. And it's not just because people would know where the women's bathrooms are, even though that would be very helpful. I think it would be a better world. I have two children. I have a five-year-old son and a two-year-old daughter. I want my son to have a choice to contribute fully in the workforce or at home, and I want my daughter to have the choice to not just succeed, but to be liked for her accomplishments. Thank you.

五、补充阅读

1）卢信朝. 英汉口译技能教程：口译 [M]. 北京：旅游教育出版社，2009.

2）苏伟，邓轶. 口译基础 [M]. 上海：上海外语教育出版社，2006.

3）仲伟合. 英语口译基础教程 [M]. 北京：高等教育出版社，2007.

测试和总结

一、测试说明

1）测试形式：
- 限时复述：考查规定时间（2分钟）内复述源语大意的能力。注意，测试有时间限制，要考虑大意和细节的平衡，并考查即兴演说的能力。
- 交传：材料为关于某主题的讲话，分为两段。做笔记并进行英汉交传。

2）成绩构成：复述占50%，交传占50%。

3）评分标准：
- 复述大意完整，逻辑清楚，用词准确；译句理解准确，信息完整，语法正确，体现逻辑关系。
- 表达流畅，少重复，少"磕巴"。
- 数字处理准确、得当。

二、测试题

1）限时源语复述

You are going to listen to an interview with Steve. He speaks with an accent typical of the southern parts of the U.S. and talks about how he felt when returning to the U.S. after living in Spain. Please listen without taking notes, and retell the message in two minutes.

生词表

英文	中文
Metro	地铁（尤指欧洲地铁）

2）英汉交传

You are going to listen to a talk titled "Tips for Studying Overseas." It is divided into three segments. Please interpret consecutively into Chinese. You can take notes.

三、评估与反思

教师评价。

主要参考文献

Engeström, Y. (1987). *Learning by Expanding: An Activity-Theoretical Approach to Developmental Research*. Helsinki: Orienta-Konsultit.

Gile, D. (2009). *Basic Concepts and Models for Interpreter and Translator Training*. Amsterdam/Philadelphia: John Benjamins.

Gile, D. (1992). Basic theoretical components in interpreter and translator training. In C. Dollerup & A. Loddegaard (Eds.), *Teaching Translation and Interpreting: Training Talent and Experience* (pp. 185-194). Amsterdam: John Benjamins.

Gillies, A. (2009). *Note-Taking for Consecutive Interpreting: A Short Course*. Shanghai: Shanghai Foreign Language Education Press.

Jones, R. (1998). *Conference Interpreting Explained*. Manchester: St. Jerome Publishing.

Moser-Mercer, B. (2008). Skill acquisition in interpreting: A human performance perspective. *The Interpreter and Translator Trainer*, 2(1).

Pöchhacker, F. (2016). *Introducing Interpreting Studies*. London/New York: Routledge.

Poyatos, F. (2001). Nonverbal communication in simultaneous and consecutive interpretation: A theoretical model and new perspectives. In F. Pöchhacker & M. Shlesinger (Eds.), *The Interpreting Studies Reader*. London/New York: Routledge.

Zhong, W. (2003). Memory training in interpreting. *Translation Journal*, 7(3).

鲍川运. 再议大学本科口译教学 [J]. 外语教育, 2008（08）: 1-7.

雷天放, 陈菁. 口译教程 [M]. 上海: 上海外语教育出版社, 2006.

林超伦. 实战口译 [M]. 北京: 外语教学与研究出版社, 2004.

刘宓庆. 口笔译理论研究 [M]. 北京: 中国对外翻译出版公司, 2004.

刘和平. 翻译的动态研究与口译训练 [J]. 中国翻译, 1999（04）: 29-33.

刘和平. 法语口译教程 [M]. 上海: 上海外语教育出版社, 2009.

刘敏华. 逐步口译与笔记: 理论、实践与教学 [M]. 台北: 书林出版有限公司, 2008.

卢信朝. 英汉口译技能教程: 口译 [M]. 北京: 旅游教育出版社, 2009.

塞莱斯科维奇, 勒代雷. 口译训练指南 [M]. 1989. 闫素伟, 邵炜, 译. 北京: 中国对外翻译出版公司, 2011.

苏伟, 邓轶. 口译基础 [M]. 上海: 上海外语教育出版社, 2009.

王斌华. 口译: 理论·技巧·实践 [M]. 武汉: 武汉大学出版社, 2006.

吴冰等. 现代汉译英口译教程（第二版）[M]. 北京: 外语教学与研究出版社, 2010.

吴钟明. 英语口译笔记法实战指导 [M]. 武汉: 武汉大学出版社, 2005.

张威. 中国口译学习者语料库的副语言标注: 标准与程序 [J]. 外语电化教学, 2015（01）: 23-30.

仲伟合，王斌华. 基础口译 [M]. 北京：外语教学与研究出版社，2009.

仲伟合. 英语口译基础教程 [M]. 北京：高等教育出版社，2007.

仲伟合. 英语口译教程 [M]. 北京：高等教育出版社，2006.